THE GAFFERS

'We have to start giving ourselves a bit more credit. We have good players and you get a bit sick and tired of the whole "well, the Irish will have a good time no matter what the result" stuff. Sure, the fans will be happy with tonight and rightly so. But we're professionals, and we have to raise our targets a bit.'
Roy Keane after a 2-2 draw in Amsterdam, September 2000

'He is immense. What must it be like to be told you're marking Roy Keane?'
McCarthy praises Keane, March 2001

'You were a crap player and you're a crap manager. The only reason I've any dealings with you is that somehow you are the manager of my country.'
Keane lets McCarthy know what's been eating him all these years, May 2002

'If you don't have any respect for me, then don't play for me.'
McCarthy's response, May 2002

'I was tired of standing up for people, supporting people. And all I would like is to be treated the way I treat people. I wanted it reciprocated and it wasn't. So I've no worries about what is happening.'
McCarthy on his decision to send Keane home, May 2002

PAUL HOWARD is the author of the best-selling, hard-hitting prison exposé, *The Joy, Mountjoy Jail – the shocking true story of life inside*, and co-author of *Celtic Warrior*, the autobiography of boxer Steve Collins. He has also written two novels, *The Miseducation of Ross O'Carroll-Kelly* and *Roysh Here, Roysh Now*, which chart the joys and woes of cult hero Ross O'Carroll-Kelly. A former Sports Journalist of the Year, he is the chief sports feature writer for the *Sunday Tribune*, and covered the World Cup in Japan and Korea for the newspaper. He lives in County Wicklow.

The Gaffers

Mick McCarthy, Roy Keane and the team they built

Paul Howard

THE O'BRIEN PRESS
DUBLIN

First published 2002 by The O'Brien Press Ltd,
20 Victoria Road, Dublin 6, Ireland.
Tel: +353 1 4923333; Fax: +353 1 4922777
E-mail: books@obrien.ie
Website: www.obrien.ie

ISBN: 0-86278-781-5

British Library Cataloguing-in-Publication Data
Howard, Paul, 1971-
The gaffers : Mick McCarthy, Roy Keane and the team they built
1.McCarthy, Mick 2.Keane, Roy, 1971- 3.Soccer managers - Ireland
4.Soccer team captains - Ireland 5.Soccer teams - Ireland
I.Title
796.3'34'0922417

1 2 3 4 5 6
02 03 04 05 06

Editing, typesetting, layout and design: The O'Brien Press Ltd
Front cover image: courtesy FAI and Eircom
Printing: Cox & Wyman Ltd

For Annie Kehoe.
Wherever you are,
you are here.

ACKNOWLEDGEMENTS

I approached The O'Brien Press in November 2001 with the idea of writing an essay examining the complex relationship between Mick McCarthy and Roy Keane and the part it played in the success of the Irish football team. Michael O'Brien and Íde ní Laoghaire said go ahead. The fact that the book was at an advanced stage when the row broke out in Saipan is a tribute to their good editorial instincts. Thank you Rachel Pierce for slave-driving me through the last two weeks of work and for a great editing job. Thank you Matt Cooper and Mark Jones for your support and guidance. Three journalists have gotten to know Roy Keane better than anyone. In their writing, Dave Hannigan, Tom Humphries and Paul Kimmage have taught me, more than anything else, what a fascinating, complex human being he is. Thank you Eamon Dunphy for saying it like it is and for phone calls putting me right. Thank you Dave Hannigan, Dion Fanning, John O'Brien, Mark McGuinness, Kieran Shannon, Malachy Clerkin and Paul Hyland for advice on the text. Thanks Mum and Dad, Mark, Vincent and Richard. Thanks to Karen and the magnificent Gormans. Thanks to Billy, Andy, Norman, Patrick and Donal and everyone at Inpho, but especially Lorraine O'Sullivan, whose outstanding photograph of *the* handshake was the inspiration behind this book.

PICTURE CREDITS

The author and publisher wish to thank the following for permission to reproduce images: Billy Stickland and Inpho for the images in the two colour sections. The copyright for all images in the colour sections belongs exclusively to Inpho; front cover image of the World Cup squad 2002 reproduced with permission of the FAI and Eircom.

THE GAFFERS

ON A DAY OF TORRENTIAL IMAGES, one stood out above all the rest. When the referee blew his whistle, Mick McCarthy stepped onto the pitch and picked his way through the stew of celebrating players, seeking out one man in particular. Out of the corner of his eye he saw him. Roy Keane, head bowed and shoulders hunched, walked in the direction of the tunnel, alone with his thoughts, a baleful look on his face carrying a warning that said Do Not Disturb. Keane had inspired a team reduced to ten men after the sending off of Gary Kelly to victory against Holland – one of the best teams in the world – and Ireland would freewheel their way to the World Cup from here. A crowd that had once booed him now chanted his name in adulation. Yet Keane looked like a man who had lost the biggest football match of his life. McCarthy saw him leaving the scene and trotted after him. He called his name and offered him his hand. Keane flashed his eyes at him for one interminable second, and then, with his eyes fixed in the opposite direction, he accepted the gesture. It was a moment so freighted with awkwardness it was difficult to watch. The architects of this team's greatest-ever performance looked like two strangers who had fallen into conversation on a bus and were saying their stilted goodbyes.

THEY'RE DIFFERENT, THIS CROWD. They're not like the players McCarthy knew in his day. They seem younger than the ones he went to the World Cup with in 1990. Boys rather than men. They're not, though. They're much the same age. But they're not men of the world like Andy Townsend was. Or Tony Cascarino, Ray Houghton, or John Aldridge. They don't sit up until the small hours dealing poker hand after poker hand, engaging in long conversations about life. They have toys instead. They have portable DVD players, digital cameras and laptop computers. They are the Nintendo generation who grew up to be professional footballers.

The bond between them all is no less close for that. They know each other intimately by now, all the little quirks and idiosyncrasies that define their places within the squad. Steve Staunton is the infuriatingly early riser, always up before Mick Byrne has to rap on his door. Damien Duff is the squad's Rip van Winkle. Robbie Keane is a knot of nervous energy. Kevin

Kilbane is such a sincere soul that the others worry about letting him out of their sight. Jason McAteer is always sending himself up to get a smile. Richard Dunne has a voracious appetite. Niall Quinn is their elder brother, mature far beyond his years yet still one of the lads.

When they're called together for international matches, they take up the best part of a floor in a hotel. They come and go from one another's rooms to try to fill up the long, tedious hours between training sessions and mealtimes. But there's one door they don't knock on. There's one door that opens only when the man who sleeps behind it decides it opens. Roy Keane rooms alone. It's the way they do it at Manchester United. He'll share with no one. He is the squad's Greta Garbo.

The rest of the team like Keane. They respect him, although the line between respect and abject terror is thin. They wonder sometimes what he thinks of them. There are times when he seems to enjoy them, shares their jokes and doesn't mind them seeing him smile. Then there are other times when he seems dismissive of them, irritated by their triviality. He will brood over a bad pass. Or someone he felt was dragging his weight in training. There isn't a member of the squad who hasn't passed his room and wondered what he's doing, what he's thinking, behind that door.

'Roy's lovely,' Jason McAteer will say, 'if only he'd talk sometimes. Or come out of his room.'

'People say he's arrogant,' says Ian Harte. 'It's difficult to get inside his head, to see what he's really like sometimes. None of us has ever really got close to him.'

'I've never really had a conversation with him,' Damien Duff admits, three-and-a-half years after they became team-mates.

Asked where they stand on the continuum between McCarthy and Keane, all of them would say they are closer to McCarthy. He is friendly, tactile, approachable.

'Not just a manager,' says McAteer, 'a friend as well.' His door is always open.

'Mick is one of the people I look up to,' says Robbie Keane. 'There are only a few managers I'd have a lot of respect for and he is one of those. Mick gave me a chance to play international football when I was seventeen years of age. A lot of people would be afraid to take that gamble. He did. Don't get me wrong, he'll have a go at you if he thinks he needs to. Whether you play well or not, he's always ready to give you a kick up the rear end, which is one of the reasons he always gets the best out of people.'

'When Roy gives you a lashing,' says Harte, 'you

wish the ground would swallow you up. But in every match you're finding out something new from him.'

'Roy doesn't say much off the pitch,' says Duff, explaining how the arrangement works between captain and manager. 'Mick does the talking in the dressing room and Roy just sits there. Then, as we're leaving, he [Roy] says good luck to us all. But then, out on the pitch, Roy's different. He's always at you to concentrate, not to give the ball away. And you think of all the big games he's played in, everything he's won, the player he is and you'd do anything for him.'

MICK MCCARTHY HAD WORK TO DO. The team he inherited from Jack Charlton in the spring of 1996 was old and going nowhere. Major surgery was required, but the neglect of underage football during the Charlton years meant there were no obvious, ready-made replacements. Nonetheless, new players had to be bedded in and older ones eased out. The culling was painful in some cases. Men with who McCarthy had shared the happiest moments of his career at the World Cup in 1990 had to be guided towards the exit. John Aldridge and John Sheridan were told they were no longer needed, as eventually was Paul McGrath. In time, Andy Townsend, Ray Houghton and Tony Cascarino went too.

The man who, more than any other player, was

the living incarnation of Charlton's route one, sledgehammer footballing philosophy showed his independence of mind by discarding the system that had brought Ireland to two World Cups and a European Championships. The New Testament, he said, would be all about passing, keeping the ball on the ground and other skills that would have been alien to McCarthy as a player.

In came a new brood of players. The public had difficulty putting names to their baby faces. There was Gary Breen, the young Birmingham City centre-half from Kentish Town in London. There was Ian Harte, the eighteen-year-old nephew of Gary Kelly, who was trying to establish himself as a defender at Leeds United. And there was David Connolly, a spry teenage striker from London whose goals kept Watford in the First Division that year. McCarthy had had his eye on him since his time as manager at Millwall when Connolly had put four goals past the reserve team. McCarthy fell into conversation with him as he left the pitch. It turned out the boy's father was from Galway and his mother from Leitrim. McCarthy telephoned Maurice Setters, Charlton's assistant and the manager of the Irish under-21 team, to tip him off. Nothing happened. When he took over the team, his memory of Connolly was jolted by a hat-trick the young striker scored in a 5-2 win over Port Vale, which helped preserve Watford's place in the First Division.

The new players would be blooded in a congested, end-of-season programme of matches, which included McCarthy's own testimonial against Celtic, friendlies against Portugal, Holland and Croatia and then what was fast becoming the customary summer trip to America, to play the United States, Mexico and Bolivia. The squad that McCarthy named was highly experimental. As well as Breen, Harte and Connolly, there were other new names to learn off: Kenny Cunningham, Gareth Farrelly, Dave Savage, Keith O'Neill and Alan Moore. After naming the players who would be travelling to Boston that summer, McCarthy ruled out any more surprises. He couldn't have been expected to foresee the future after all.

On the second Saturday in May, Roy Keane inspired Manchester United to victory over Liverpool in the FA Cup final, the second instalment of the Double. Afterwards, he spoke about his plans for the summer.

'I'll take a few weeks' holiday and then report to Dublin for the Ireland matches,' he said. 'I've missed a lot of internationals in the past few years because of injuries, suspensions and other reasons. But Mick has new ideas and it's an exciting time to be involved with Ireland. We want to do well in the US Cup and I want to play in the games.'

His words were balm to McCarthy's worried mind. When he took the job, Keane was the one recalcitrant piece he thought would not fit into the jigsaw. His high rate of absenteeism raised doubts about his commitment to Ireland. He played in only three of Ireland's eleven qualifying matches for that summer's European Championships, pulling out with short-term injuries and minor niggles, which, in some cases, had cleared up by the following weekend. Keane had no problem playing for Ireland. But he disliked Charlton, as a manager and as a man. Rightly or wrongly, he saw McCarthy as a chip off the same block.

Keane and McCarthy played on the same Ireland team just twice during the thirteen-month overlap in their international careers. As players they weren't close. It was their personalities more than the generation gap. They were just wired differently. McCarthy was the dutiful headboy to the master Keane didn't respect. Keane would sit at the back of the bus and sneer at the way McCarthy always sat with the manager. The joke was that he was after the job. To McCarthy, Keane was part of a new element in the Irish team who didn't regard the manager with the respect he deserved. Charlton seldom had to remind the older players that there was a disciplinary code in force. They were given enough slack to enjoy themselves, but knew better than to pull against the chain.

On the summer tour of America in 1992, however, Keane did and all of the simmering tensions between him and McCarthy came to the boil. The last match of the tour was in Boston. With Charlton away for the day, Keane was one of a group of players who decided to kill the time before their overnight flight at an Irish bar in the city. As the pints kept coming, the flight home seemed to matter less and less. Afternoon slid into early evening and there was no sign of the players back at the hotel. McCarthy had been left in charge of the team, as he always was in Charlton's absence. He was furious. He ordered the bags of the errant players to be loaded onto the bus and asked the driver to stop at the pub on the way to the airport to pick them up.

It was a job convincing them to leave the pub. McCarthy began to take the whole business as an affront to his authority and he went for the group's sneerer-in-chief. When Keane, messy after his day's drinking, climbed onto the bus, McCarthy started shouting at him. 'Look at the state of you,' he said. 'Have you got no respect for yourself? Where's your professionalism?'

Keane's retort cut McCarthy to the bone: 'Where's your first touch?'

Only they know what resentments were left to incubate during the years that followed. McCarthy never played for Ireland again after that summer, and the adhesive that once bound the old players together slowly melted away.

At the World Cup in the USA two years later, Keane was involved in another row, this time not as a protagonist but as a bystander hit in the crossfire. Charlton was away one afternoon and had left Maurice Setters in charge of training. In the oppressive Florida heat the players were forced to sweat through an old-fashioned routine involving a lot of legwork. Most of them thought it was doing more harm than good. Andy Townsend told Setters what he thought and there was a sharp exchange of views. Word reached the ears of the press that Keane had been involved. Charlton used the confusion to pretend there had been no row. Charlton, his face an angry shade of red, frogmarched Keane into a press conference and asked him, in front of the media, 'Roy, did you and Maurice have a row?' Keane's answer was a casual 'No', but he never forgave Charlton for what he made him do that day. Telling a half-truth just to suit Charlton's agenda undermined Keane's sense of being his own person. It was a seminal moment not just in his relationship with Charlton and Ireland but also in his development as a man.

Charlton had to make do without Keane for most of his final days in charge of Ireland. But McCarthy needed him. Keane knew what it took to win football matches at the highest level. To the youngsters being exposed to the frontline of international football for the first time he was a hero, and he was the pivot around which McCarthy planned to build his new team. When Townsend retired injured from McCarthy's first match in charge, against Russia, he didn't need to be told who to pass the captain's armband to.

Keane, a man defiantly free of sentimentality, probably wouldn't have cared to know that at the age of twenty-four he had become the youngest man ever to skipper Ireland. And, as if to throw the honour back, he got himself sent off at the end of the game for kicking a Russian substitute, Omar Tetradze – the sort of petulance for which he was becoming famous. McCarthy pointedly refused to look at him as he left the pitch. Keane returned to England immediately, flown home by Manchester United. But McCarthy's need to keep him onside could be seen in his apparent ambivalence towards the incident.

'No manager can condone a player who deliberately kicks another,' he said, 'but every manager will understand how players, in the heat of the moment, react to a bad tackle.'

ON 23 MAY 1996, on the Tuesday of his testimonial week, McCarthy reached out to Keane again by naming him his captain for the summer tour of the USA. The responsibility, he hoped, would make Keane feel more involved and curb his more temperamental urges. Forty thousand people turned up at Lansdowne Road for McCarthy's benefit game, Keane was not one of them. Worse still, he hadn't telephoned McCarthy to ask to be marked absent. His non-appearance cast a pall over what should have been one of the happiest days of McCarthy's career. Instead of discussing his eight years playing for Ireland, helping to undo England at the 1988 European Championships and leading Ireland into the last eight at the World Cup in 1990, he found himself answering questions about a player who had very publicly jilted him on his big day.

In the post-match press conference, McCarthy said he didn't know where Keane was. He had tried all weekend to contact him, and even on the day of the match, but he couldn't be found.

'I have not had even a phone call about Roy,' he said, 'and at this stage of our development that is disappointing. A message was communicated to the FAI in midweek that he had a hamstring problem, but apart from that there has been no contact. I'll now have to start looking for him.'

McCarthy was joined in his search by just about every national newspaper in Ireland and Britain. Tongue-in-cheek headlines appealed to members of the public to come forward with information. An English tabloid newspaper chartered a helicopter to fly over his stg£1.5m home in the stockbroker belt in Cheshire, hoping to snap a shot of him in his garden. Journalists flew to the Italian island of Capri where he was rumoured to be holidaying.

Keane's rebuff was just the latest blow to McCarthy's authority in his first tentative months as Ireland manager. Word had slipped out of Merrion Square that he hadn't been everyone's first choice for the job. FAI president Louis Kilcoyne admitted during a radio interview that he wasn't top of his wish list. Then he had problems securing ratification for the appointment of his old friend, Ian Evans, as manager of the under-21 team. On top of that, he'd lost his first two matches in charge, to Russia and the Czech Republic. And now at a time when he needed to win the respect of his young team, a player in whom he had made a very public declaration of faith was cocking a snook at him.

'I'm putting no deadlines on Roy's arrival,' McCarthy said, putting his best face on. 'He is one of the best players in England and I want him in my team.'

To appreciate the depth of McCarthy's annoyance with Keane, it helps to recall the circumstances in which his own international career began. He was called onto the Irish squad in May of 1984 for a friendly match against Poland in Dublin, followed by a meaningless summer tournament in Japan, which would have the team traversing nine time zones for just one full international, against China. There would be no caps awarded for the other games scheduled against a local university side and a Brazilian club side. And McCarthy had the perfect out: his brother, John, was getting married and he'd agreed to be his best man. He could have walked away without ever being troubled by what-ifs and what-might-have-beens. Eoin Hand, the Irish manager, had three centre-halves – David O'Leary, Mark Lawrenson and Kevin Moran – who were infinitely more gifted than McCarthy. At a push, with the complicity of injuries, he figured he could win no more than a dozen caps. And what kind of a man would miss his brother's wedding? McCarthy weighed it up and did what his heart told him. John was told to find a new best man. But then, McCarthy and Keane were different.

The weekend of his testimonial match, McCarthy had to suffer the indignity of a conversation with a hoaxer claiming to be Keane. It was all turning into an unseemly business.

On Tuesday, 30 May, Keane was found at the rained-off, one-day match between Lancashire and Gloucestershire at Old Trafford, enjoying the corporate hospitality. Listening to the radio phone-ins the next day, it was possible to believe that Keane had committed an act of sedition, the fact that he was watching a cricket match – a garrison game, of all things – adding a perverse twist to the story.

On Wednesday night, three days after the storm broke, Keane finally said his piece, not in a phone call to McCarthy but in a statement issued by his solicitor. No mention was made of a hamstring injury, rather it claimed that Keane was tired after a long season and had telephoned the FAI to announce that he was withdrawing from the squad. As an attempt at self-justification, his defence was self-exculpatory and self-condemning at the same time. While stressing that he enjoyed a good relationship with the Irish manager, the statement was released to the Press Association without McCarthy being told. It flashed up on the news wires, in fact, while Ireland were playing Portugal at Lansdowne Road.

After seeing his team lose to an injury-time goal, McCarthy made his way to the cramped band room at the far end of the ground for the post-match press conference, eager to talk about what had been a stout performance by his young players. When the subject of Keane was broached, he clasped his hands together, indicating that the book was closed. He was asked what he thought about Keane's statement. He said he had heard nothing about any statement, then listened in appalled silence as selected parts were read to him by members of the press.

'Roy Keane,' it said, 'regrets the publicity which has arisen during the last few days following his request to be excused from the fixtures which the Irish international team are playing during the summer. Such a request on his part was no more than that made by several other senior members of the international squad following an arduous season in the Premiership. Contrary to statements made in some sections of the media, there is no absence of commitment on Roy's part to playing for his country, which he regards as the highest honour for any sportsman. Furthermore, he has an excellent relationship with his manager, Mick McCarthy, which he would not like to see damaged by the recent adverse press reports.

'In an effort to avoid further inaccurate press comment, Roy would like to make it clear that, prior to leaving for Italy following the FA Cup final for a few days' holiday, he endeavoured to make contact by telephone with Mick McCarthy. But when his efforts proved unsuccessful, a message was left with the

Football Association of Ireland. It is Roy's earnest wish that he now be left to enjoy, with his family, a few weeks' break from football and to resume playing for his country in a few months' time in the World Cup qualifying competition.'

McCarthy couldn't conceal his anger. 'I said all along I want to speak to Roy,' he said. 'I don't want to see his solicitor. No way. Shall I get my solicitor to write to his?' Pressed on the substance of Keane's claim that his request to be excused from the end-of-season programme was communicated to Merrion Square, he said: 'Who requests the players to come out? Who is entitled to a request: me, or a ticket-seller in the FAI, or whoever? I have to tell you, if there was a request to the FAI, Mick McCarthy would have received that request and I didn't. So you can decide what you want from that. Do you take my point? Why are *you* telling me that? If I want to tell somebody something, I walk up to them or pick a 'phone up and tell them. That's the way I do it. But then again, I'm an abrupt, straightforward, to-the-point gentleman. That's how I do it.'

The following day, still seething, McCarthy stripped Keane of the captaincy and deleted his name from the party travelling to the USA. Speculating on Keane's future, he said, with a degree of pessimism, 'I need him to show the desire to play for his country. If

I see that, I will deal with the situation again. I am not saying the door is still open to America for him, because I've named my squad of twenty for that trip and Alan Kernaghan is coming with us instead of Roy.

'The lads who reported for duty and worked so hard in training over the last couple of weeks deserve some respect. I have no intention of chasing people to come and play for Ireland. Either they turn up and play or I get on without them. It's as simple as that. I'm not suggesting that the players who didn't turn up are lacking commitment. What I am saying is that people should be breaking their nuts to play for Ireland.'

An unnecessary argument, conducted over poor lines of communication, opened up an unbridgeable fissure between Keane and McCarthy. Both asked for a curtain to be drawn on the whole sorry farrago, but they were now two men at vastly different coordinates, who would never enjoy anything more than a cool working relationship from that point on.

IT WAS IN ALL INNOCENCE that an Iranian journalist asked Mick McCarthy to talk about the difficulties he had as an Englishman trying to motivate a team of Irish players. For a moment it looked like McCarthy would tackle his inquisitor like he had a generation of

English centre-forwards. It was a question that cut right to his heart. You can criticise his ability as a player, say he was a carthorse who had no business keeping David O'Leary out of the Ireland team for three years. You can question his ability as a manager, call him a tactically naïve chancer who was allowed four years of on-the-job training by the FAI before he got it right. But don't, under any circumstances, question his Irishness.

So for thirty unconscionable seconds he stared the reporter down, while those who knew McCarthy shifted uncomfortably in their seats and looked into their notebooks. For once, though, he tackled the question without taking out the man as well.

'Say if your father left Iran,' he said, 'because he couldn't get work at home. And he ended up going to England, where there was lots. And say if your father had a son who grew up in England, speaking English with an English accent. Now, does that mean the boy isn't entitled to call himself Iranian?'

Substitute Ireland for Iran and the hypothesis is McCarthy's life story in distillate. Emigration played a huge part in shaping not only his own life but also the Irish team he played for in the 1980s and 1990s and the one he manages now. He is a man with a highly developed sense of who he is and where he is from. His father, Charles McCarthy, left his home in

Tallow, County Waterford, 'poor as a church mouse' in the lean years after the Second World War to look for work in the Yorkshire mines. He got clever, though, and eschewed the pits for a healthier life driving for a local engineering company in Barnsley. He met and married a local girl and their children were brought up to consider themselves half-Irish. It was on the Rec (a piece of land opposite the family home), as McCarthy often nostalgically recalls, that his father taught him how to kick a football and hold a hurley.

In March 2001, during a two-stage trip to Cyprus and Andorra halfway through the qualifying campaign, McCarthy's father passed away. It had been Charles's final wish that his son should continue with his preparations for the two matches. So McCarthy had said what he knew would be his last goodbyes to his dad before he set off. The strain on him that week was enormous, but he did his grieving quietly.

'The old fella would want me to get on with the football,' he said at a press conference when condolences were offered.

The quiet dignity with which he bore his loss moved everybody. Eight months later, on the night in Tehran when his team qualified for the World Cup, he didn't need to say who the tears he shed were for.

It's a side to him that he hid for a long time. Most of the stories McCarthy likes to tell to define himself invariably involve confrontation. Someone who was rude to him in the street perhaps, or someone who called him names in the dressing room: 'Do you want to step outside, pal?' Bravado is the hard ectoskeleton he uses to protect himself. He is much more sensitive than he will ever admit. With the press he plays the part of the bluff North of Englander, answering even the most innocuous questions with a prickly, offended tone. But even among those journalists he counts as his enemies – those 'outside the tent pissing in', as he puts it – there is a genuine fondness for the man and his simple decency. Loyalty is his core value. He met his wife, Fiona, on his first day at school. He has no designer friends. Most of those he calls his mates have been his mates for a long time. He is a brilliant *raconteur*, with the timing of a professional comic. Humour – two brands: sarcastic or self-deprecating – spills out of him.

It can be difficult to reconcile the image of McCarthy as the down-to-earth, good-natured man with the more churlish side to his personality that is occasionally revealed. He has made an art of rubbing people up the wrong way. When Denis Irwin was still one of the best full-backs in the Premiership, he dropped him for Jeff Kenna for a friendly against

Argentina. Before he sent Irwin on as a second-half substitute, McCarthy told him to prove himself. Irwin, the most decorated Irish player ever, had nothing to prove to McCarthy, or to anyone else. A year later he became the newest member of a growing club of players who retired from international duty on bad terms with the manager.

As a player, McCarthy was the symbol of an era. 'Six foot two, eyes of blue, Mick McCarthy's after you,' was the popular terrace paean to him, though he wasn't everyone's idea of a dependable central defender. The most eloquent descriptions of the kind of player he was came not from Dunphy, who called him 'a boil on the arse of Irish soccer', but from McCarthy himself: the man who said, 'I've always said that if my granny was clean through I'd have kicked her'; the man who patented the phrase, 'Nobody ever scored a goal from Row Z.' At Italia '90, he committed more fouls than any other player and in his autobiography, *Captain Fantastic*, seemed almost pleased to relate the news.

The man who led Ireland out against England in Cagliari that summer has never had a problem admitting that, as a boy, he watched the World Cup final in 1966 with more pride in the part of him that was English. He was seven years old and mad about football, to the point where his schoolwork suffered. He wasn't gifted by anyone's reckoning. He had a trial at Barnsley at the age of sixteen. But even standing five feet, ten inches tall with the beginnings of a full beard he failed to get himself noticed. After leaving school early, he resigned himself to a life as an apprentice electrician in the very mines his dad had tried to warn him away from. But with the bloody-mindedness that became the hallmark of his career, he returned to Barnsley via a few outings with the reserve team. The offer of a contract came a few days after he had sat the pre-selection test for his electrical apprenticeship. McCarthy ended up learning his trade at the nearby Oakwell Football Ground and not the nearby colliery.

After Barnsley, he moved to Manchester City, helping them to win promotion to the old First Division. It was there that he was first marked down as officer class. His manager, Billy McNeill, noticed that whenever he solicited the players for their thoughts before matches, it was always McCarthy's arm that shot in the air first. And it was always his booming sergeant-major voice that carried through the early morning air at training. McNeill and McCarthy didn't always get on. McCarthy's bite was too often worse than his bark. McNeill handed him the captaincy and he got himself booked needlessly in his first match. McNeill was furious. He pulled him aside and told him he'd made a mistake. What had he been thinking when he put him in charge of the team? he asked. In a startling echo of a far more public row sixteen years later, McCarthy told the manager to shove the captaincy. But they quickly made up. It was a product of McCarthy's salt-of-the-earth, working-class upbringing that he liked to bring his rows to a close quickly, man to man, with a brief exchange of views and a handshake.

When City were relegated – as they inevitably always are – he couldn't face returning to the Second Division, particularly when he didn't have to. Celtic were interested in him so he moved, with his young family, to Scotland. He must have feared he'd made a catastrophic mistake when David Hay, the manager who signed him, was sacked three days later, but McCarthy needn't have worried. His new boss, it transpired, was Billy McNeill.

He became a terrace idol at Parkhead. The fans had been hankering for a tough, uncompromising centre-half ever since McNeill had retired as a player himself. In McCarthy, they got one. They still speak in reverent tones about his performance against Werder Bremen in the European Cup, when he kept Karl Heinz Riedle quiet and helped earn Celtic a scoreless draw. He'll be forever worshipped too for the header he scored against Rangers in the semi-final of the

Scottish Cup, which kept them on course for the Double in 1988.

By then he'd surprised himself by winning thirty-four caps. His international career evenly straddled the end of the Eoin Hand era and the beginning of the Jack Charlton one. Hand gave him his début against Poland in 1984. He looked ten years older than the twenty-five declared in the match programme, his brown hair already flecked with grey, with an impossibly fecund moustache dominating his large, open face. Even his nose, which would become a favourite prop in his after-dinner repertoire, lost the battle for notice with his golden-brown bristles. Ireland had more top-quality centre-halves than they knew what to do with, and in terms of talent McCarthy was at the back of the line. His expectation was a dozen caps. But Hand liked him. And Charlton loved him. McCarthy was the remedy to his lifelong distrust of ball-playing centre-halves. He didn't like, as he put it, the 'fannying around' that the soon-to-be-exiled David O'Leary did at Arsenal. In McCarthy, he found just what he was looking for: an old-fashioned, no-frills defender who would help him put his hoof-and-hope long-ball tactics into effect. As a man, Charlton liked him too. They had shared the same local just outside Barnsley long before their paths ever crossed in Ireland, and they had sometimes talked about football over a pint.

McCarthy, then, was a predictable choice to captain the team at the World Cup in Italy in 1990. The match that epitomised the reasons why was against Spain at Lansdowne Road in a qualifier in 1989. When McCarthy shook hands with Emilio Butragueno in the centre circle before the match, he looked like he was ready to tear the Spanish striker's arm out of its socket. He put on a magnificent display of leadership that afternoon to shut Spain out. Booked early on for marking Sanchez Monolo a bit too literally, he spent the entire day harrying and hustling, refusing to let Spain string more than a couple of passes together and throwing his head, or a hefty size-eleven at any ball that came near him. He was inspiring. 'Hyper' was the word he chose. Near the end, the frustration got to Butragueno. After one tackle, he screamed 'McCarteee' and made a lunge for him. McCarthy caught him by the chin and marched him away. Ireland won one-nil and eased their way through to their first ever World Cup finals.

Loyalty was always an important principle with McCarthy, but it was from Charlton that he learned the value of it as applied to football. In the summer of 1989 he made an ill-advised move to French First Division side Olympique Lyon. He had impressed a lot of people with his performance against Spain and the move, he hoped, would set him up financially for life. But he struggled in France, with the language as much as the football. Six months before the World Cup he wasn't playing regular football. Charlton stood by him. He picked him when McCarthy knew he'd no business playing international matches. He got out of France, agreeing to a loan spell with Millwall that would give him regular football. He remembered how indebted he felt to Charlton and he marked it down. It would inform almost everything he did when he became manager.

By his own admission, McCarthy was never 'one of the lads'. He was closer to Charlton than he was to any of his team-mates, which explains why, as captain, he had a sharper sense of *politesse* than Roy Keane would have. When the players arrived in Rome for the quarter-final against Italy that summer, they were horrified when they saw the size of their hotel rooms. Two single beds had been squeezed into rooms that comfortably accommodated only one. After four weeks on the road they had accumulated a lot of luggage. There were double rooms in the hotel, but the FAI officials had them. McCarthy was asked by the players to sort it out. He went to Charlton, who told him he had a double room and was prepared to give it up. Setters gave up his room too, and eventually the officials were persuaded to give up theirs and move to another hotel. The FAI didn't just turn into a house of bunglers in 2002.

'Another mess-up,' McCarthy wrote in his auto-biography. 'We are here to play in what is the most important game in Ireland's history and we have got off to a bad start.'

Italia '90 was a defining moment in Ireland's modern history, one of those where-were-you-when moments. Ireland reached the last eight. For ninety minutes they stood on the brink of a place in the semi-finals. They came up short against Italy. It was no disgrace. McCarthy trudged back to the dressing room and cried for twenty minutes. The thousands of fans who had travelled to be there wanted one last curtain call from the players. His team-mates went back out, but McCarthy sat there, slumped in his grief like a drunk at chucking-out time.

'And that's *my* regret,' he says, 'not going out onto the pitch after the game. I wasn't bothered at the time. I didn't like getting beat. Never did. Still don't. But we gave it everything we had that night. And I shouldn't have regretted a minute of that match.'

He's much less inclined to hide his sentimentality now. Managing Ireland has taught him the value of it. The national anthem is a case in point. As a player he never bothered learning it. '*Sinne Fianna Fáil/ Atá faoi gheall ag Éirinn.*' They were empty words that meant nothing to him. Then he got a video cassette in the post. It was from a man who had watched McCarthy's young team line up for matches and was disturbed by how few of them seemed to know the words. They should know it, he said. And though he hadn't thought about it much before, McCarthy agreed with him. The cassette was an instructional video on how to sing the song, complete with a lyric sheet written in phonetics. McCarthy watched it a couple of times and decided it could help foster team spirit. So he called the players into a room and they watched the tape together. Afterwards, with song sheets in their hands, they sang it together. It sounded awful. But he could sense the passion. Every time they reached the final few bars, a couple of voices would break away from the rest and shout, 'Come on, fucking Ireland!'

ON A COLD, SQUALLY DAY IN NOVEMBER 1996, Roy Keane arrived in Dublin wearing a mane of black curls and the beginnings of a beard, his unkempt appearance in seeming deference to his role as pantomime villain. He was back to play for Ireland against Iceland at Lansdowne Road. Six months had passed since he had failed to show his face for McCarthy's testimonial and the end-of-season friendlies; eight months since his sending-off against Russia, the last time he played for Ireland. McCarthy had won the popular vote, but Keane wasn't about to accept the sackcloth-and-ashes treatment. After training with the team in Clonshaugh, he was asked by an RTÉ reporter whether he cared that his commitment to his country was being called into question.

'No, not really,' he said. 'I don't care what people think. It's all sorted out between me and Mick. I had a private chat with him and we sorted it out. What was said remains private. I missed two games through injury and then withdrew from the USA Cup because of a private matter. That's all in the past.'

Much had happened while he'd been away. The loss against Portugal was followed by another against Holland, and only a Niall Quinn equaliser against Croatia ninety seconds from time rescued them from the precipice of an unprecedented sixth successive defeat. The summer tour of America brought the usual mixed bag of results. They lost 2-1 to the United States. They drew 2-2 with Mexico in an off-the-wall match in New Jersey that saw stand-in captain Liam Daish sent off and McCarthy and Quinn ordered from the bench. Three days later they beat Bolivia 3-0, McCarthy's first victory since taking over. The youngsters played well on the trip. It was with more than just a sense of mischief that McCarthy said the older players who spent the summer at home would have difficulty winning back their places.

On the last day of August, with Keane again missing – this time recovering from knee surgery – McCarthy mixed old players with new when Ireland travelled to Liechtenstein to begin their qualifying campaign for the 1998 World Cup. The tiny principality in the Rhaetian Alps was a place that many of the players had hoped never to see again. The previous summer, in the qualifiers for Euro '96, they were held to a goalless draw, a result that marked the beginning of the end of the Charlton era. The ignominy of the result was best captured by Peter Ball of the *Sunday Tribune*: 'Ireland drew with a mountaintop yesterday.' This time around an early goal led to an avalanche, with Ian Harte celebrating his nineteenth birthday by scoring the fourth of Ireland's five goals.

In October, with Keane still missing, Ireland beat Macedonia in Dublin, Jason McAteer adding the punctuation mark to an emphatic three-nil win with one of the best goals Lansdowne Road has ever seen. Keane wasn't missed at all. When the stadium announcer mentioned his name at half-time, a chorus of boos rippled around the ground. It was a forewarning of what was to come when he made his return against Iceland the following month.

McCarthy had begun flirting with the new wing-back system that had become *de rigueur* on the Continent, using the experienced triumvirate of Andy Townsend, Ray Houghton and Alan McLoughlin as the bedrock of his midfield; Denis Irwin, Gary Breen and Steve Staunton as his central defence; with Harte and Jeff Kenna operating as attacking full-backs down the flanks. Days before the match against Iceland, Staunton got injured. It wasn't McCarthy's week. Quinn had just telephoned to confirm his worst fears about the injury he'd picked up a few weeks earlier. He'd snapped his cruciate ligaments, an identical injury to the one that had kept him out of the World Cup in 1994, except this time it was the other leg. He needed an operation and would be missing for the guts of a year. It was bad news, but McCarthy would make-do and mend. The loss of Staunton was a bigger blow. Instead of revising his tactics, he made up his mind to push Keane back into the centre of defence, a position he had filled before for Manchester United. Matthias Sammer had played in the same role for Germany at Euro '96 and had been the star of the tournament. Keane, McCarthy felt, could be even better.

But the first time he touched the ball a section of

the crowd started booing. No one in the press box could remember an Irish player being barracked by his own fans before. It continued for about twenty minutes, adding an even sourer flavour to one of those days when nothing went right. It was clear early on that McCarthy had erred. The player that Iceland feared most was put in a position where he could do least damage. By sacrificing Keane's aggression in midfield, he had surrendered the initiative to what was a poor, injury-ravaged Icelandic team, and they were allowed to escape with a goalless draw.

McAteer was lucky to stay on the pitch as long as he did, having been repeatedly spoken to by the referee. Four months later, fortune claimed its forfeit. Ireland were beaten by unfancied Macedonia in Skopje, with McAteer sent off for an appalling karate-style kick on Artin Sakiri. McCarthy was already facing an uphill struggle to get Ireland to the World Cup in France; suddenly the gradient was pitched even more steeply.

The only good news that could be salvaged from the detritus of what was turning out to be a disastrous year was that Keane looked like he might grow into his role as the leader of McCarthy's young team. Not only did he cope with the baiting against Iceland, he ran himself to a standstill trying to inspire those around him. The news that the press had named him as their Man of the Match was greeted by a polite round of applause. McCarthy must have hoped it would persuade him to come home more often.

ALL GENIUSES HAVE THEIR DARK SIDES. Roy Keane's lurks in his shark eyes that never seem to fix on anything and the thick vein that throbs on the side of his forehead. It's in his faintly threatening skinhead and the urgency with which he walks, as if trying to burn off some manic energy. He is the player whom most Ireland fans connect with and the one they know least about. He guards his privacy with an angry jealousy. Everybody wants to get close to him, but few ever do because most of the qualities that make him the man he is are elusive. He is un-pigeonholeable. A shape-changer. An enigma. The moment you think you've got him taped, he does something to unravel all your cosy conceptions.

The most popular caricature of him is as the brilliant but unstable midfielder whose frustrations often find their voice in violence. He has a febrile temper. His sensibilities work on a hair-trigger. All will be well with him, his team sailing along on cruise control, and then someone will put in a mistimed tackle, a misplaced word and, red with anger, he'll react. The malevolence of his rages can be frightening. It's probable that even he himself doesn't know what damage he would have done to Alan Shearer last year had David Beckham not held him back. And only he knows what silent fury was building in his mind in the years before he caught up with Alf Inge Haaland – the player he associates with the blackest time in his life – and stamped on his leg with such ferocity it was a wonder it didn't break.

He has spent so many years creating a monster out of himself that the man is often misjudged. It's only recently that Keane has started to show the subterranean layers of his personality. He is not a monster. At least, not all the time. He has a large and colourful palette of moods. He can be warm, convivial, engaging and then, by turn, shy, moody, taciturn. In interviews he can be diffident to the point of being monosyllabic, his responses reflexive, those dreaded pillars of football-speak – 'at the end of the day', 'all credit', 'tremendous' – framing everything he says. Then, when the mood takes him, he will disarm you with long, intelligent, passionate homilies about football and the world.

He is never quicker to speak than when he feels someone around him is giving less than their best. He wants the folkloric one hundred and ten percent from everyone and no one has been spared the snake-lick of his tongue. He has rowed with Mick McCarthy. He has accused the FAI of being amateurish in the way it does its business. He has called his Manchester United team-mates 'an average' team. He has berated the silent majority who fill Old Trafford for home matches, parodying them as simple event-goers who are too full up on prawn sandwiches to get excited about the football. He has, according to legend, raised his voice to Alex Ferguson.

As hard as he is on other people, Keane is even more unforgiving of himself. Such is the intensity he brings to his work that you have to ask sometimes if there's not some form of madness driving him. He plays football with the troubled genius's pursuit of perfection. Sometimes he finds it. In 1999, by sheer force of his desire, he dragged United into the final of the European Champions League, single-handedly inspiring a comeback from two goals down against Juventus at the Stadio de Alpi. He scored the galvanising first goal and never let up, even when he picked up a yellow card that ruled him out of the final. It was, said Ferguson, 'quite simply the most emphatic display of selflessness I have ever seen.'

There have been other performances to compare with it. He has saved some of his best work for Ireland. Against Portugal in Dublin he was like a chess grandmaster, playing five or six different games simultaneously. Then he did it all again against

Holland three months later. There wasn't a flicker of happiness on his face afterwards. Like most great artists, satisfaction is a sentiment he rarely expresses.

He was, by his own estimation, useless in school, yet he possesses a sharp intelligence. He is curious about the world around him and is an avid reader of books. The joke at Old Trafford is that he buys them as a device to avoid talking to his team-mates on long-haul flights. That's football. The culture is grounded in a devout anti-intellectualism. Only someone as certain of himself as Keane would admit to preferring the company of a good book to engaging in brain-dead conversation with other players.

His role as United captain doesn't extend beyond the white-lined confines of the football pitch. He is team captain, not club captain. Gary Neville looks after the social side of the job for him, arranging the go-kart races, the paintball games and the other events aimed at improving team spirit. Keane doesn't do it. It's not him. And as a consequence the word 'loner' has fastened itself to him like a mollusc. Of all the words that have been found for him, this seems to hurt him more than any other. He isn't a loner, he argues, he just has no high-profile friends.

If he has drawn a firm demarcation line between himself and his team-mates, it's because he abhors the shallowness and vanity that goes with being a footballer in this media age. Whereas David Beckham has embraced the celebrity lifestyle that comes with his station in life, Keane feels imprisoned by it and only really feels free when he's at home with his wife and four young children, or back in Cork with his *real* friends. He was one of only two United players who skipped the Beckham wedding. He didn't show up to the FAI annual awards dinner in 1999. And his record for turning up at testimonial matches isn't too good either.

For all his hurt at being portrayed as a recluse, there are times when he wears his remoteness like a badge of honour. Asked to contribute a couple of anecdotes to a documentary about his old team-mate and room-mate Denis Irwin, he made a point, once the camera was rolling, of saying, 'Me and Denis were never that close.' He told another journalist about the day a few years ago when Mick McCarthy came to his house to discuss a team matter and added, with some degree of pride, 'And you know that *nobody* gets into my house.'

At the same time he is capable of the sincerest acts of generosity. There are too many stories about his kindness for him to keep the lid on this aspect of his personality. One of the staples of the Irish team's preparation for matches in Dublin is the shopping trip to Grafton Street on the afternoon before a game. Keane never goes. The crowds put him off. He usually does what shopping he needs in the first half-hour after the shops open, a baseball cap pulled down low on his forehead to keep the world at one remove. While the rest of the Irish players are dropping thousands in the city centre, Keane will flit out a side door of the team hotel and head to a hospital to visit sick children. An untold number of charities in Manchester have also benefited from his money and his time. There are no novelty-size cheque presentations for the benefit of the local media. It's done quietly. No fuss.

There are times when it's wise to handle him like a live grenade. His down time is his and he guards it irritably. Fans who take photographs of him when he's on holidays will receive *the stare* and a sharp lesson in where the parameters lie, delivered in language of varying hues of colour. After Ireland played in Cyprus last year, Keane was having one of his quiet moments in the airport departures lounge, sitting apart from the rest of the players, staring intently out the window at the runway. A drunk was lumbering from player to player, demanding their signatures on an old, greasy Italia '90 cap he was holding. Keane was the last. Some of the players wondered whether they should warn him to leave Keane to himself. He staggered over to him and asked for his autograph.

Lost in his thoughts, Keane didn't hear him. The drunk nudged him with his elbow. The photographers who were there didn't know whether to get ready for a scoop, or to take cover. Keane stared him down for a few seconds, then signed the cap, without there being any international incident.

He can laugh at this side of himself: the demon that people see when they look at him. Most of the advertisements he's done have hammed up his 'bad boy' image. Diadora announced its boot deal with him on billboard posters that featured a picture of Keane with his eyes reddened out and the slogan, 'We've sold our soul to the devil.' There's a Kit-Kat ad in which he is seen peacefully doing some embroidery in the dressing room with classical music playing in the background; the Barclaycard ad where he glowers at Angus Deayton for ordering a prawn sandwich; the Walkers crisps ad where he tries to bite Gary Linekar's hand off.

And just when it looks like he might be lightening up, he'll try to take Shearer's head off or dismember Haaland. Perhaps the one image of Keane that will endure the longest is the one of him chasing referee Andy Durso to berate him about a decision he had made. There were other United players in the mob, but Keane's anger seemed to be so much deeper; his neck muscles straining and his skin cinched tight around his eyes, which protruded like a couple of eight-balls. A week later, he was asked about the incident.

'He kept running,' he explained. 'If he'd just stood still, we wouldn't have had to keep chasing him.'

He regards this side of his personality like some troublesome kid brother he can't but be fond of. He falls out with so many of his team-mates on the training ground, he says with typically self-deprecating humour, he can never remember from day to day who's talking to him and who isn't.

Any effort to understand Keane and the forces that drive him must begin with the ten months of his career he was forced to sit out in 1997 and 1998. It was a black period in his life, but also a watershed. He injured himself swinging a careless leg at Alf Inge Haaland the first time they met, when Haaland was with Leeds. Keane heard his cruciate ligament tear and knew he was in trouble. It's an injury that ends careers. He sat out the season, contemplating the thought that at twenty-six years of age he might never again be the player he was. He watched Arsenal win the Premiership and the FA Cup Double. It depressed him. He took to weight training with a religious zeal. Two and three hours after the rest of his team-mates had clocked off for the day, he was in the gym at Old Trafford, focusing on his comeback. Paranoid about putting on weight, he stopped drinking and cut chips and other fatty foods out of his diet. He offloaded twenty pounds of excess cargo, his year of abstemious living revealed in the chiselled face and heavily contoured body he showed off on his return.

The transformation in Keane wasn't only physical. There was an almost Hydesian change in his personality, too. Having glimpsed the end, he decided that for whatever time remained he was going to get the most out of himself. For almost a year he worked with masochistic intensity to get himself fit again. Energy is never destroyed, just converted into another form. He re-channelled his into making himself a better player and making better players of those around him. He would say in interviews that the trophies he had won meant 'literally nothing' to him, but he played like they meant everything. His desire to win was frightening.

'It taught me a lot,' he said last year, reflecting on that period of his life. 'In a crazy way, it possibly was the best thing that ever happened to me. It made me step back and realise what I had and what I nearly lost and it made me enjoy my football even more. I had taken it all for granted – all the glamour, the money, everything about football.'

Yet that was understandable. The old Keane – the

drinker, the sybarite, the star of all those 'nightclub incidents' that filled the hungry maw of the tabloids – was reacting as any young man might after having money and fame thrust his way so unexpectedly. The story that had him writing to every league club in England as a teenager, looking for a trial, is probably apocryphal. But it is true that any of the scouts who came across him playing for Rockmount in Cork considered him too small to become a professional footballer. He was nicknamed The Boiler Man for his ability to get things moving in midfield. He was a brilliant schoolboy player, but when he went for a trial for the Ireland under-15 team, he heard the familiar refrain: not big enough. For a long time, it didn't look like he would make it.

He left school as soon as he legally could. All he wanted was to be a footballer. But living on a local authority estate in Mayfield, in a city still reeling from the Ford and Dunlop factory closures, it was the spectre of a lifetime of unemployment, or at the least low-paid unskilled work, that hung over Keane as he grew towards his late teens.

In 1989, when most young players with his kind of talent had found themselves apprenticeships in England, he drifted into the League of Ireland, the league where big dreams usually go to die. He signed for Cobh Ramblers and started a FÁS course that was based on the English football apprenticeship system. From Monday to Friday he trained in Dublin, then returned to Cork at the weekend with £60 in his pocket to play for Cobh. In February 1990, a few months before Mick McCarthy led Ireland out against England at the World Cup, an unexpected twist of fate turned Keane's life around. He was playing in Dublin in an FAI Youths Cup replay against Belvedere. Noel McCabe, who scouted for Nottingham Forest, watched the match and told his employers to get the lad to England before some other club found out about him.

So they did. Keane flew through the audition and, at eighteen, signed for Forest. Brian Clough gave him a quick and memorable baptism. Forest were playing at Anfield. Steve Hodge was injured. Keane was helping to lay out the kit in the dressing room before the match when Clough uttered the famous words: 'Irishman, put the number seven shirt on. You're playing.'

'At one stage,' Keane would recall later, 'I was running back and Steve McMahon was running next to me. I remember looking at him and thinking, "This is it."'

Keane was fortunate to have a disciplinarian like Clough as his first boss. He knocked some of the rougher adolescent edges off him. He sent him home from one summer trip to the Channel Islands for mis-behaving, and threatened to sell him to a circus if he ever repeated the somersault he executed after scoring a goal against Norwich. Clough never frightened Keane like he did other players, though.

'It baffled me the way some of the established stars at Forest got into a panic every time he was around the place,' he once said. 'I was never afraid of him. I got on with him and if he said something I disagreed with, I'd tell him.' It was all a rehearsal for the future.

If he got lucky with his first boss, he was even more fortunate with his second. Alex Ferguson was an admirer from literally the first minute he saw him play.

'They [Forest] came to Old Trafford to play us,' he once said, 'and when the ball was kicked off, it went back to Bryan Robson. Keane comes flying through and absolutely cemented him. I'm sitting there thinking, "That's a bit cheeky, coming here and tackling like that."'

When Forest were relegated, Ferguson paid stg£3.75m to get Keane after deciding that here was the rock on which he would build his team. The deal was done over lunch and a game of snooker in the manager's house.

In his nine years at Old Trafford, Keane has developed into arguably the best footballer in the world. Certainly there are more naturally talented players, but it's difficult to think of any with his range of gifts. Zinedine Zidane, Rivaldo and Luis Figo all have their charms, but they are not, on their own, match-winners. Not since Diego Maradona has a player won so many important games on his own. Maradona did it with the sheer witchery of his skills. Keane does it by the force of his desire. He is Manchester United's and Ireland's best defender and best attacker, the one player whose absence diminishes both sides. He carried Ireland to the 2002 World Cup on his back, just as he carried United to the final of the European Champions League in 1999. And three years later, two aggregate goals adrift of Bayer Leverkusen in the second leg of the semi-final, it was Keane alone who kept playing to the abject end.

Under Ferguson, he also became a firebrand. He was never sent off in his two years at Nottingham Forest and was booked only once in his first twenty-nine matches for Ireland. But as the stakes increased, so did the Football Association's disciplinary file on him. Perhaps his most oft-referenced sending-off came after he stamped on Crystal Palace's Gareth Southgate in an FA Cup semi-final, an act of stupidity given that the murder of a Palace fan had foreshadowed the game. Realising his value, Ferguson indulged Keane like he did no other player, preferring to see his moments of madness as evidence of his commitment rather than malice. Their admiration for one another never goes unreciprocated.

Forgiving McCarthy for not being Ferguson has taken Keane a long time. He liked McCarthy little more than he liked Jack Charlton, which is to say not at all. He missed all but a handful of Charlton's last twenty matches in charge of Ireland and, for a whole myriad of reasons, played in just one of McCarthy's first ten. For a long time the myth persisted that Keane had 'never done it for Ireland'. After his performance against Spain in Seville in 1992, no less a judge than Maradona described him as the best young midfielder in Europe, while RTÉ viewers voted him Player of the Tournament at the World Cup in 1994. He has seldom played a poor match for his country, but his frequent no-shows divided people on the question of his commitment to his country. He once said on an RTÉ documentary, 'Have Boots, will Travel': 'When people ask me where I'm from, I always say Cork, never Ireland. It's always Cork first and Ireland second.'

Over the years, whatever hostility Keane and McCarthy felt towards each other was leavened by pragmatism. McCarthy wanted to go back to the World Cup finals as a manager and Keane wanted a second opportunity to showcase his talents on football's biggest stage before he retired. It didn't matter if they didn't get on. They made an effort to work together. When they needed to talk, they usually communicated through an intermediary, mostly Mick Byrne, the assistant physiotherapist. And for a long time it looked like it might, just might, all work out for the best.

Keane inspired Ireland to new heights in the qualifiers for the World Cup. Most of the matches were characterised by the sight of him bawling out his team-mates, telling them he wanted more from them. The serious side to Keane's personality was making demands off the field as well. He was unable to bite his lip any longer on the subject of the team's training facilities and travel arrangements. At United, Keane was flying in comfort. On the journey to Cyprus with Ireland, the sight of FAI officials sitting up in the first-class cabin while the players sat with their legs cramping up in the economy seats annoyed him too much to stay quiet about it.

Keane gave an interview to Paul Kimmage of the *Sunday Independent* in which he criticised the FAI for the amateurish way they prepared for big games. He attacked the officials for taking the best seats on the airplane and said the team's training pitch at Clonshaugh was a disgrace. They were the kind of issues, he said, that would persuade him to retire early from international football. It wasn't the way

McCarthy had prosecuted the cause of players' rights when he was captain, but it worked. When the team travelled to Estonia ten weeks later, the players sat in the premium seats at the front of the airplane while the officials sat remorsefully back in steerage. The embarrassment was a small price to pay to keep Ireland's best player happy. But the question of whether McCarthy or Keane was in charge of the team crossed more than a few minds.

NIALL QUINN TURNS OFF THE MAIN ROAD and into a small estate of middle-of-the-market semis with neatly manicured lawns, family saloons and the null air of a dormitory suburb in the middle of a working day. The short detour is a means of illustrating an argument he's making. Not so long ago, he worked here. It used to be Roker Park, the home of Sunderland Football Club before they traded up to the bigger and brighter Stadium of Light.

'Over there, where that house is,' he says, 'if my guess is right, that was the spot where I scored my very first goal for the club.' The car slows to a crawl.

'I've come up here a couple of times now and driven around, trying to see if there's anything of the old ground left. There's nothing. It was one of the oldest football grounds in the world. You'd think they would have left a turnstile, or a terrace step, or, I don't know, a wall with the name of the team on it. But nothing ...' And there, neatly captured, is the point that Quinn has spent half this February morning making: football is changing at such a fast rate that nobody ever stops to notice what's being lost.

There are few players as grounded in their earth as Niall Quinn. He's glad he's the age he is, happy that retirement isn't far away and thankful that his career straddled football's boom-time. He's old enough to remember the days when his weekly wage was measured in hundreds, yet young enough to have given the tree of plenty a good shake. The result is a man who is comfortable materially, but has a humility that is uncommon in his line of work.

Football was a dowdy, doomed-looking business when he decided to make a career of it in 1986. He joined Arsenal at a time when football was dull, crowd numbers were falling and hooliganism blighted the game. Within a decade it had changed irrevocably. Paul Gascoigne dissolving in tears at Italia '90 was the iconographic image that did more than anything else to help football reinvent itself as part of mainstream popular culture in England. It happened at a time when clubs were being forced to spend millions of pounds upgrading their stadiums in the wake of the Hillsborough disaster in 1989. The new all-seater stadiums, plus Sky TV's imaginative re-branding of the game sold it to a bigger and better-heeled audience.

Money was suddenly sloshing about the place. Clubs could afford to put foreign marquee players on their payrolls, adding to the game's *chic*. Football was the new rock 'n' roll, its players exerting a fascination that transcended what they did on the field. They could become millionaires while still in their teens without having to work as hard as Quinn's generation did. Formal education for most of them ended when they were fourteen or fifteen, yet they were earning four- and five-figure sums every week, often without having the intelligence, or the maturity to handle it. American football and baseball have provided enough signposts to show where that particular road leads.

'If you care about football and you're honest, you'd have to be worried about the game and where it's going. It's in fifth gear now, absolutely flying. But it wouldn't be inconceivable to think that another two years of what we've had this year and people will turn their backs on it. And what will accelerate that is players not caring about the game and rubbing people's faces in it.'

The names of Lee Bowyer and Jonathan Woodgate are skulking around the edges of the conversation, as are the Chelsea players who jollied it up in drunken oblivion the day after September 11.

'Football is unrecognisable from the way it was ten years ago. And along with all the rewards that have come in, there's the problem of being in the public eye more. I have to say how much I admire David Beckham. He handles it impeccably. But there are those who can't handle it. And they don't understand how they're affecting the game in general.'

Few players could deliver such an anguished jeremiad on the state of the game and get away with it. Quinn has put himself in a unique position. His decision to give away the stg£1m his testimonial raised to two children's hospitals is the good-news story that football has craved for a long time. It has captured a mood. Tony Blair, his local MP in Sedgefield, namechecked him in Prime Minister's question time, describing him as an example to Britain's youth. The Sunderland fanzine *A Love Supreme* has started a campaign to get him the freedom of his adopted city. He didn't set out to become some post-millennial Bob Geldof, but he understands why he has struck a chord.

'There's been so much bad publicity surrounding footballers that there was an appetite for something like this.'

The game is so awash with easy money that the players are losing their connection with the audience.

'I think what has to happen, if we're to get

football back in good nick again, is that the players are going to have to start thinking for themselves a bit more. There are lads in our dressing room whose agents pay their bills for them. The gas company and the electricity company and the 'phone company, they send their bills direct to the agents. So there are footballers who don't know how to pay a gas bill. It's incredible. You can see where the agents are coming from. They're handling it so the players can concentrate on their football and be free of pressure, which is the theory. But if you take away the cogs, the nuts and bolts of everyday life, then it all becomes meaningless. And as we've seen, the devil makes work for idle hands.'

He doesn't spare himself from criticism. He counts himself among those guilty of abusing their privileged lives. 'I find myself in situations where I get invites to every big do that's on in the North of England. I go racing and I get brought to the champagne bar. I go shopping and they give me discounts that I need less than anybody. If my car needs servicing, they come and collect it, whereas everyone else has to go and drop it off at the garage and then come back to collect it.

'And in terms of where I've overstepped the mark, I'd love to tell you I'm the kind of bloke who finishes training and comes home to play the family man. I'm not. If the pub's still open and the drink's being served, I might as well not have a watch. And then the next day, for my troubles, I've to do an hour-and-a-half work and I come and have a sleep in the afternoon. That's the biggest privilege of all. And the wife will go, "Will you give me a hand with the kids?" and I'll go, "No, I've got a game on Saturday. I've got to rest." And she'll say, "You weren't thinking about that at four o'clock this morning." Then I'll say, "I needed to get my mind off things." I can justify anything. But when I look in the mirror I tell myself, "You've abused this."'

Handing over his testimonial money was his way of settling his arrears. He decided to do it a long time ago, the 1980s he thinks. It wasn't much of a decision. He never thought there'd be a testimonial. An undertow of insecurity told him he was never going to be anything more than a journeyman footballer. Every day of his six years at Arsenal, he wondered when the ride would end.

'The best line I ever read about myself was by Tom Humphries. He said that Niall Quinn had been to Fortune's kitchen and licked all the pots clean. And that's exactly how I feel. On my school team, there were better players than me. I'm not saying that just for something to say, I'm saying it because it's true.'

Somewhere along the way he learned to appreciate himself. His move to Manchester City helped. The elephantine touch of his early years disappeared, along with the foal-like ungainliness in his legs. More and more he focused on the things he was good at. His first World Cup helped. He went to Italia '90 as Jack Charlton's third-choice striker, but was given a chance for the final group game against Holland. Ireland were a goal down with twenty minutes to go and looked like they were coming home. Then Packie Bonner punted a typical long ball forward. Berry van Aerle watched the flight of it and, when it came down, tried to cushion it back to Hans van Breukelen. But the Dutch goalkeeper spilled the ball right at Quinn's feet. 'Probably the easiest goal I ever scored for Ireland,' he says, but also the most important. Without it, there would have been no penalty shoot-out against Romania – that defining moment in our modern history – no heroics against Italy in Rome, no quarter-of-a-million people shoehorning themselves into Dublin city centre to welcome the team home.

The goal launched his international career. For the next eleven years he was Charlton's and McCarthy's first-choice striker, except when he was injured, which was usually at the most important times. Late in 1993, he suffered the first of two potentially ruinous cruciate injuries and missed the World Cup in the USA the following year. He recovered quicker than the doctors had predicted and declared himself fit enough to play in the tournament, but Manchester City wouldn't let him. He didn't bitch about it and still doesn't. He just looks back on it with the philosophic outlook of a man who twice in his career sat down to read his insurance policy and debated into the small hours about whether it was time to cash in his chips.

His last World Cup seems like a lifetime ago now. He can't believe he's going to another one, to neatly bookend his career. It isn't just the pain is his back that has him feeling his age these days. When he listens to Robbie Keane and Damien Duff talk, it dawns on him how many of his team-mates had still not made their Confirmation when he played at Italia '90.

'Robbie drives me mad,' he says. 'He remembers the words to 'Give it a Lash, Jack', 'The Boys in Green', all those silly songs that came out back then.'

He's still young enough at heart to laugh when he feels his mobile phone slide down his leg and realises that Jason McAteer has cut the pockets out of his tracksuit again. These players have given his career a booster-shot of enthusiasm. He's seen this new generation grow up under Roy Keane's tough love and McCarthy's gentle care. He remembers that when he first joined the Ireland squad in 1986, he couldn't look Liam Brady in the eye. And he noticed that most of the younger players were the same way around Keane.

'I wasn't just in awe of Liam Brady. I was over-awed by him. I was afraid to make a mistake in front of him. Even off the pitch, it was a long time before I could relax in his company. And looking around, I think that's what happened with this team. A lot of players were a bit too anxious around Roy, as though they didn't really believe in themselves.'

For Quinn, it explains why Ireland failed to reach the European Championships in 2000. They beat Croatia and Yugoslavia, two of the best teams in the world, and needed only to hold on to a one-goal lead in Macedonia to win the group.

'We saw the finish line and panicked. They got an equaliser from a corner with, what, a minute to go? We ended up in the play-offs, drew Turkey and we all gulped. If we had to play them now, we wouldn't gulp. We'd fancy it. That's how much this team has grown up.'

The dynamic between McCarthy and Keane has been the biggest factor in that. 'It's not something that's planned though,' he says. 'They don't sit down and say, "I'll be like this with them and you be like that." It's just something that works. I think Mick has a huge respect for what Roy does on the football field. He's a monstrous performer and never stops looking for the ball. And I think Roy has a huge respect for what Mick has tried to do with the team, in terms of changing the emphasis of playing a target man up front and launching everything at him.'

Does it matter that they're not friends, or that Keane isn't close to anyone in the squad?

'Well, I look back at the old Ireland team and none of us really became best friends for life. People might think we did, but we didn't. There might be a guy you played at the same club with who you might stay in contact with, maybe two or three others you'd ring very occasionally over the years to see how they are. But none of us are going to be bosom buddies at the end of this. It's not how it works.

'We'll always have a connection, just as me and Mick will always have a connection because of Italia '90. But I wouldn't run to Mick with my troubles. Or Roy wouldn't run to him with his troubles. Some of the younger players might because he's brought them through. But as they get older they won't anymore. That's the way it is. We don't need to be friends.'

IT WAS KEANE WHO SET THE TENOR of the World Cup campaign on the night it began. The team was drawn in the same group as Holland and Portugal, both semi-finalists at Euro 2000. McCarthy's decision to start with the two most difficult assignments, in Amsterdam and Lisbon, seemed like an act of compassion to put the country out of its misery quickly. The smart money had him looking for a new employer by Christmas.

As if he hadn't problems enough, Mark Kennedy and Phil Babb, two players who owed McCarthy big performances in Holland, woke up on the first day of the week of the match in a cell in Bridewell Garda Station in Dublin. They had been arrested outside a nightclub on Harcourt Street after causing damage to the roof of a woman's car. The woman, it transpired, was a garda. After they were charged and released on bail, the two players were promptly thrown out of the squad.

The loss of Babb forced McCarthy to gamble on Richard Dunne, a rookie who had never played a match of such importance. In Kennedy's stead he took a chance on McAteer, an unpredictable player who tended to suffer from rushes of blood to the head. For over an hour that night they gave Holland a masterclass in the art of passing.

'They toyed with us,' said Louis van Gaal, the Dutch manager.

Robbie Keane scored with a header from six yards in the first-half, and then in the second-half McAteer paid out on McCarthy's wager with an exquisitely struck goal from outside the box.

With twenty-five minutes to go, the Dutch rallied. Ireland defended with asinine stubbornness, desperate to hold on to what they had. But goals from Jeffrey Talan and Giovanni van Bronckhorst gave Holland an undeserved share of the points. Dunne saved a certain winner for Holland in the last minute when he prostrated himself at Patrick Kluivert's feet.

Leaving the Amsterdam Arena that night, the Irish players wrestled with conflicting emotions. They couldn't decide whether they should be grateful for the point they'd won, or angry about the two they'd let slip away. McCarthy, while disappointed, saw the glass as being half-full.

'I'm proud of the team because we came here to take Holland on at their own game,' he said. 'We passed the ball and played with controlled aggression. I'd have taken a draw before the start.'

Keane dwelt on what had been spilt. 'We have to start giving ourselves a bit more credit,' he said. 'We have good players and you get a bit sick and tired of the whole "well, the Irish will have a good time no matter what the result" stuff. Sure, the fans will be happy with tonight and rightly so. But we're professionals and we have to raise our targets a bit. We haven't qualified for a major finals since 1994 and you get into this rut. Sometimes the players even underestimate themselves.'

It was an amazing speech. And it was epoch-making. The friction between the manager's bright, positive outlook and the captain's splenetic way of looking at the world became the dynamic force that drove the team forward. Warming at last to the job of leading his country, Keane spent the next thirteen months ramming his message home, exhorting his team-mates to play above themselves, be better, dream bigger.

BROOKFIELD CELTIC WERE GIVEN THE KEYS to their new container on a frostbitten Wednesday afternoon in January. The lifespan of the last one was indecently short. The local junkies got in and turned it into a shooting gallery, until someone dropped a bottle of petrol and a lit match through the hole in the corrugated iron roof and put the place out of its misery. The local children had to change in and out of their gear on the sidelines all season. Not anymore. It's another of Marie Green's minor miracles.

She knew nothing about football when she set up the club three years ago. She couldn't have picked Mick McCarthy or Roy Keane out of a line-up, but she did know Robbie Keane, Anne Keane's young lad, from around the corner in Glenshane. His career in England was the talk of the estate and the local kids were turning cartwheels out on the road – damaging themselves some of them – trying to imitate his goal celebrations. So, using Robbie-mania as bait, Marie Green set up a football club. St Vincent de Paul agreed to kit out the team and the local nuns helped her lean on the men in the estate until a manager and a coach stepped forward.

It's hard work and sometimes it saps her spirit. If ever she asks herself whether it's worth all the trouble, she need only look at the tramlines that the joy-riders have left across her pitch, the used condoms that litter the sidelines, the palimpsest of graffiti that covers the walls in the area and the bars erected on the local shop as a redoubt against ram-raiders to be reminded just how much her efforts matter.

But, as she says herself, that's the over-publicised downside of Tallaght. The newspapers aren't much interested in positive stories, like how a community so devastated by unemployment, crime and drug abuse can also be the most fertile ground in the country for producing professional footballers; how two of the current Irish team kicked their first ball no more than a five-minute drive away from The Square.

Robbie Keane's house isn't difficult to find. 'It's up the top of the road,' says a wiry eight-year-old, the approximation of a grin playing on his lips, 'the one with the Weatherglaze.'

Just around the corner, no more than a hundred yards away from the Keane family's new front door, is the home of Jason Gavin of Middlesboro. Robbie, though, spent most of his boyhood hanging around in the Cloonmore estate across the road, where his friend Ian Bradley lived. Ian's kid brother, Stephen, signed for Arsenal on the day of his sixteenth birthday. Barely of an age to shave, he knocked back Alex Ferguson who flew to Dublin to try to persuade him to sign for Manchester United.

Among Bradley's neighbours are Mark Mulraney, who spent time at Millwall, and Niall Byrne, who was on the books at Liverpool for two years, while just across the river in Drumcara is the home of Graham Gartland, a teenager on the fringes at Barnsley. On the far side of the dual carriageway sits Killinarden, the estate where Manchester City defender Richard Dunne was born, while back down the road, on the other side of The Square, is Kilnamanagh, one of Tallaght's first private-housing developments, which has five sons playing football in England, including Graham Barrett, who captained Arsenal to the FA Youths Cup two years ago, and Keith Foy of Nottingham Forest.

It's a rich harvest. The joke in Tallaght is that it

must be something in the pylons, though the truth has more to do with boring demographics and socio-economic factors.

'The old cliché is true,' says the Irish youths manager Brian Kerr, 'that Foxrock doesn't produce many footballers and Tallaght doesn't produce many sailors. Football has always been a game for the working classes and this is an enormous working-class community we're talking about here.'

Tallaght was Dublin Corporation's solution to the chronic shortage of housing in the city of Dublin in the late 1970s. Though a city-sized suburb today, for the first ten or fifteen years of its life it was nothing more than a series of sprawling, maze-like estates and giant prairies of open fields in the green foothills of the Dublin Mountains. There was, among the people who moved there, a sense of being cut adrift, of being dropped into a wilderness to fend for themselves. Richard Dunne's father, Dick, feared he'd made a mistake from the day he arrived.

'It was in the middle of nowhere,' he says. 'There were no what you would call facilities. There wasn't much of a bus service and there were no shops. Anything we wanted, we had to buy out of these mobile shop vans.' Richard learned to play on the half-acre patch of grass in front of his house.

Keane's parents moved into the newer Glenshane

estate a few years later, when Robbie was still a baby. 'There wasn't anything for him to do growing up except play football,' says Anne. 'There was nothing but fields. And that's what him and his friends did all day. They kicked a ball around.'

Ireland played in their first World Cup while Keane and Dunne were still in primary school. The first time they knew Mick McCarthy, he was the Italia '90 sticker that nobody wanted. Number one hundred and seventy-eight. Everyone had three of him. But during that balmy summer the team that he captained branded itself into the imaginations of Keane and Dunne and tens of thousands of other youngsters.

McCarthy, Quinn and Paul McGrath were Robbie Keane's first idols, while Dunne wanted to grow up to be an attacking midfielder like Ray Houghton, or Ronnie Whelan. His size militated against it. He had weighed into the world at a whopping nine pounds and two ounces, and was six feet, two inches tall at the age of sixteen. At Home Farm it was diplomatically explained to him that, genetically, he was built to be a defender. Italia '90 was a watershed moment in his life.

'The whole area went mad,' he says. 'There was bunting hanging from every house. We all sat in and watched the matches. At half-time we were out kicking the ball around the street for fifteen minutes, then it was back in for the second-half. And lads you hadn't spoken to in ages, you were stopping them and pulling this big pack of stickers out of your pocket and asking them did they have any swaps.'

It wasn't only Italia '90, an abundance of fields and the want of anything better to do that steered so many youngsters like Keane and Dunne towards football. Where their parents came from was as much a factor. Because Tallaght was a Dublin Corporation production, the population it was built to accommodate was drawn mostly from city areas like Crumlin, Drimnagh, Walkinstown and The Liberties, all of which had strong footballing traditions. The Keanes and the Dunnes both moved from Crumlin, as did Gavin's father and Bradley's mother.

'The people who were involved in football in these areas brought their expertise with them,' says Kerr.

Dunne's uncle, Theo, the former manager of UCD, sensed that something was stirring fifteen years ago. 'I was a sales rep. for Tayto,' he says, 'and that was my area. And I'd often stop the car next to a field and watch a match. You could see that the level of skill was much better than you'd see anywhere else.'

Yet the best young players had to leave the area to be successful. Dunne was travelling across the city to Home Farm from an early age, while Keane left local side Fettercairn for Crumlin United, another of the country's leading schoolboy sides, once he realised how good he was. Few scouts ever venture out as far west as Tallaght to watch football, though many eventually find themselves in living rooms in the area, making pitches on behalf of English league clubs.

With Shamrock Rovers putting its roots on a site opposite The Square, there is hope that Tallaght will one day develop a schoolboy side to rival the great football nurseries. The only cloud in the sky is the upturn in the economy. When Ireland played in their first World Cup, male adult unemployment in estates like Glenshane and Killinarden ran as high as seventy-five percent. In a perverse sort of way, it was a great resource. Since the economic boom that figure has been falling steadily, but so too has the number of local men with time to devote to football.

'The Celtic Tiger has been good for Tallaght, but not good for football in Tallaght,' says Liam Perry, secretary of St Maelruan's, the second biggest club in the area. 'There was a time when managing a team was what occupied a lot of men in this area who were on the dole. Now there's so much work around, it's difficult to get bodies.'

St Maelruan's fielded ten teams last season, but could easily have put out ten more had they had more coaches. Liam turned away more than a hundred kids and it broke his heart. Bored children are prey to other temptations, a truth underlined when his under-14 team are forced to move their cup match against Naas to another venue because a stolen car has demolished their goalposts at Bancroft Park.

Marie Green may not have four Irish trialists on her team, but just like Liam she believes every boy in the area should have the chance to play football. There might not be a Keane, a Dunne, or a Gavin among her lot, but she'd settle for just saving one from a life of trouble. That and maybe just the frisson of excitement that comes over the estate whenever Robbie comes home and the kids are out on the streets again with their plastic footballs, jumpers for goalposts, under the street lights, improvising around parked cars, team line-ups constantly changing as old players go off for their dinners and new ones arrive, the scores well into double figures as bedtime approaches, wondering whether *he* might pass by any minute and – you never know – join in.

GOOD DAYS AND BAD DAYS, Kevin Kilbane greets them all with that infectious, gap-toothed optimism of his and it's almost possible to believe him when he says the vitriol doesn't bother him. People who've been going to Sunderland matches for forty years and more say they've never seen a player so cruelly eviscerated by his own fans. He's booed when he's named in the start-ing line-up and booed when he's named on the bench. New terms of abuse are invented for those occasions when he gets off it. 'Fuck off back to Cowland,' was a recent offering.

Ireland has become his place of refuge, interna-tional match weeks a safe asylum from his mistreat-ment back home. It was Mick McCarthy's belief in him that sustained him when his belief in himself was running low. It would have been easy for McCarthy to stop picking him, were it not for his fealty to the principle that players who've done a job for him in the past are owed something. Such sentimentality is rare among football managers. McCarthy stood by him during his worst days and his reward was some of his best.

When he arrives at Dublin Airport, Kilbane breathes out. In Ireland, he can be himself. There's nobody telling him he's a waste of money, nobody telling him his eyes want testing. There's nobody sending him into a nervous flap whenever the ball comes his way. It's a world of paintbox colours, where everything is simple and uncomplicated. Kilbane is, in the argot of the game, a confidence player. When the feedback is positive, he'll do what he does best. He'll receive the ball in midfield. His left arm will semaphore a fake movement and, instead of playing a pass, he'll suddenly drop his shoulder and cut outside, beat the full-back for pace and drop a cross onto the head of a team-mate in the penalty box. When Niall Quinn broke the Irish goal-scoring record with his header against Cyprus, he had Kilbane to thank for making it easy for him.

Playing as well as he did that night only makes it worse for him when he returns to Sunderland. 'You can do it for the fucking Paddies, but you can't do it for us,' someone will shout from the anonymity of the crowd. And his touch is suddenly poor. His passes find the feet of opposition defenders. His crosses leave the radar.

'You can go into matches,' he says, 'telling yourself that you'll do this and that and win them over, but it never works out. If you spend your whole time thinking about what you have to do to impress them, then it never comes off. It's only when you relax and enjoy your football that everything falls into place.'

It's easier in theory than in practice. Last year, a local newspaper 'revealed' that he wears glasses when he goes shopping. The punchline was inevitable.

'I've got broad shoulders,' he says. 'I'm big enough and strong enough to take it. And I'm confident enough in my own ability.'

But behind the chirpy front the hurt is clear. So spiteful was the abuse last year that his manager,

Peter Reid, began using him only in away matches.

'Everybody would have understood if Mick had dropped me during that time, but he didn't. And I owe him for that.'

Playing for Ireland was a dream his father instilled in him. Farrell Kilbane was born on Achill Island and, like many of his generation, moved to England to escape the economic depression of 1960s Ireland. In Preston he met Theresa, from Kenagh in County Longford, who'd made the same trip. They got married and had children and raised them with a keen sense of their Irishness. The local church and the GAA club were the umbilical cords that connected them to home. Farrell played Gaelic football in the Lancashire leagues, while Kevin served on the altar at the church where Alan Kelly went to Mass every Sunday. Kelly kept goal for Preston and was soon to be Packie Bonner's understudy with the Irish team. Kevin got to see his first hero close-up when he got a job as a ballboy at the club.

He was still in school when Ireland played in the World Cup in Italy. The day McCarthy led Ireland out against England, he singled himself out by wearing his ill-fitting Republic of Ireland shirt into class.

'It was the way with so many other footballers, I think. You're a kid and you see your team playing in the World Cup and, from that moment on, that's all you want to do in life.'

When he started to make his name as a professional footballer, his allegiance hadn't changed. Sam Allardyce, his manager at Preston, summoned him to his office one afternoon to tell him he'd earned a call-up to the England under-18 squad. Kilbane said he wasn't interested. Allardyce wondered if the boy realised what he was saying. He himself had toiled his entire career himself, dreaming of a chance to play for his country and now some ingrate stood in front of him, blithely turning down the opportunity.

'You see, England's not my team,' Kilbane told him in his bubbly Lancashire accent. 'I want to play for the Republic of Ireland.'

Allardyce ordered him out into the February frost to think about what he was saying. He was eventually persuaded to go to Lilleshall for the experience. Allardyce hoped that the thrill of training with the England youth team would change his mind. It didn't. When he realised the boy wasn't going to be turned, he telephoned McCarthy who, he'd read, had just replaced Jack Charlton as manager of Ireland.

'There's a kid here you need to take a look at,' he told him. Ian Evans pencilled Kilbane's name into the under-21 team to play Russia a month later.

England continued qualifying for the big

tournaments, while McCarthy's nascent Ireland team kept coming up short. Kilbane was there for the near-misses and then, finally, the breakthrough. He suspected that a corner had been turned in September 2000. They travelled to Amsterdam for the first match of the campaign with a sense of giddiness he hadn't felt before.

'It was like we were all brothers together. We'd been through so much, so many disappointments, and we were going there to get a result. We were unfortunate not to win, but we got a point, which was the most we would have hoped for beforehand. We grew up that night. As players and as men. It was the first night we felt that we'd arrived, that we were finally the team that Mick had been working to build for years.'

And Roy Keane never let them stop believing. 'He's a man mountain. A great leader. He lifts you when you see him going on his runs, when he's going from box to box, when he's getting on the end of passes, when he's scoring goals. But it would be wrong to say we're a one-man team. No one relinquishes responsibility. We work for each other. Which is why the team is better than its individual parts. If someone's not pulling their weight in there, they know they're going to get a bollocking.'

From Keane? 'More often than not, yeah. He'll

often tell me what he thinks of me at any particular time. But it's not just Roy. I've had bollockings off Robbie Keane and I've had bollockings off Niall Quinn. And if Roy's not passing to me, I'll tell him what I think of him.'

A brave man.

A MONTH AFTER IRELAND PLUNDERED a point in Amsterdam, it was clear that Keane had become a law unto himself within the Irish squad. At the beginning of October, they travelled to Lisbon for what looked like being the most difficult qualifier of all: the away match against Portugal. The players were told to report to the team hotel in Dublin on the Tuesday, five days before the game. Keane breezed in on the Wednesday, a day late. McCarthy, in foul humour, had to stand up in front of the press and admit that, once again, he didn't know where his captain was. It can't have escaped Keane's attention that he was in a far stronger position now than he had been in 1996. It looked like he was lording it over McCarthy.

Training began half an hour late on Wednesday while they waited for Keane to arrive. When he did, he put it down to another breakdown in communication. 'The fact is,' he said, 'that I left a message with somebody in the FAI and it doesn't seem to have been passed on.'

It was the old excuse and it prompted questions about what kind of relationship Ireland's manager and captain had. Did Keane not have McCarthy's mobile number? 'At the end of the day,' he said, 'Mick [and] Mick Byrne have my home number and if there's any problem, they can always ring me. But nobody rang. It's a bit of a farce because I had a dead leg going back to the PSV match [the previous week].'

This time, unlike six years earlier, McCarthy accepted it at face value. 'A message from Roy got mislaid somewhere along the line between the FAI and United,' he told a press conference. So vital was Keane to the team's chances of reaching the World Cup finals that McCarthy was prepared to indulge him.

'McCarthy and Keane At War,' the *Evening Herald* headline screamed in eighty-four-point type on the front page. They weren't quite there yet, though. McCarthy was still in Neville Chamberlain mode. But at a time when almost every journalist in town had bought the line about a mutual respect developing between them, it was a remarkably prescient piece of journalism. The McCarthy and Keane relationship had gone past the frosty stage, the newspaper said, communication between the two had broken down.

And then, in a casual comment made in an interview, Keane undermined McCarthy again. Phil Babb and Mark Kennedy, the two banished players, should be allowed back into the squad, he said. They'd served their punishment.

The following Saturday, Keane helped Ireland bank another point with a 1-1 draw against Portugal. The next time he turned up late, it hardly merited a mention. It was becoming obvious that if he could have gotten away with flying in just for the matches, he would have. Given the state of their relationship, it might not have been a bad idea.

STEVE STAUNTON IS A GRUMP. He says so himself. Grumpy is his default mood. There are very few times when he's not grumpy, though there are degrees of grumpiness. When he's not playing he's an angry grump, banging on managers' doors, wanting to know why. When he is playing he's a happy grump.

He is his own man, as determinedly independent as the superhero chin and the steely blue-eyed stare suggest. They tell a story about the time he joined the Ireland squad back in 1988. A quiet teenager from Dundalk with wavy blond hair, some mistook his silence for shyness. There was a natural order to things in those days. There were team leaders and *domestiques*. The rule was that you deferred to your elders until you were an elder yourself and there were new kids around to defer to you. Not Stan. He put his head around a door one day and found a card school in session. Liam Brady looked up from his hand and told the boy to fetch some tea and biscuits. Staunton told him to get his own fucking tea and biscuits.

Respect isn't something you pay him in instalments over a period of time. He demands it now, up front and in full. With his put-down of Brady, he got it. Nobody took liberties with him after that. McCarthy loved him, catching reflections of himself in his prickly independence of character and low tolerance threshold for bullshit.

He doesn't say much more than he needs to, carefully rationing his words. It makes sense. He's the son of a garda. He is deeply distrustful of journalists. 'You boys,' he calls them, or sometimes, 'you lot,' his hostility clear. Journalists wrote him off, tried to pension him off before he was ready to go.

He doesn't see it, but it was understandable. Things went awfully quiet for him for a while. Most careers build slowly towards a crescendo. With Staunton, all of the good stuff came at the start. He had won a league championship and an FA Cup with Liverpool by the age of twenty. At twenty-four he'd played in two World Cups. Liverpool sold him to Aston Villa. He kept improving as a player albeit out of the spotlight. Then he made the mistake of going back to Liverpool. It didn't work out. He couldn't hold down a place in a team that had stopped winning trophies. He went back to Villa – no money changed hands for him – but couldn't get a game there either. Ian Harte took his place on the Ireland team. And all that remained was for him to shuffle off and join his old friends from Italia '90 in retirement. Only he knows how close he came to making that call to McCarthy.

Then a convergence of circumstances threw him back onto the boards again. An injury epidemic struck down most of Ireland's centre-halves and Staunton was asked to fill in for the match against Portugal in Dublin. The groans were audible when the team was read out over the public address system.

'Too many people had forgotten how good a player he was,' says Niall Quinn.

But when did it happen? When did euphemisms like 'great servant' and 'utility player' suddenly start attaching themselves to his name?

'What happened to Steve Staunton, basically, was that he went back to Liverpool,' says Dave Woodhall, the editor of the Aston Villa fanzine *Heroes and Villains*. 'When he left this club he'd matured into a brilliant player, either in defence or midfield. He had his limitations. He was never a great tackler or a great header of the ball. And he wasn't what you would call a stopper. But he could always pass his way out of trouble. One time he hit this incredible ball with that left foot of his and the next day the *Birmingham Evening Mail* compared him to Liam Brady. But when he came back to Villa the second time round, you could see the deterioration. We got him on a free transfer, but you could hear everyone asking why we'd bothered taking him back.'

Returning to Liverpool was the wrong move for the right reasons. Money was a factor. But more than that, going back was his way of righting the wrong that was done when Graeme Souness let him go in 1991. Souness admitted it was the biggest mistake he made during his short time in charge of Liverpool. He hadn't half as many regrets as Staunton, though, who'd just bought his first house in Merseyside when Souness showed him off the premises. The fact that he regularly name-checked his old team in interviews convinced many Villa supporters that a piece of his heart remained at Anfield.

When he went back there, Villa supporters grieved over their loss. Then the decline set in. Better players than Staunton were affected by the depression that hung over Liverpool. English football's meanest defence became English football's most comical, and he couldn't hold down a place in it.

'All I can say is that at the time it was the right

thing to do,' he says of the move now.

Manager Roy Evans suddenly decided that what he needed was a hard-tackling stopper and Staunton was never going to pass that audition. There was a succession of half-remembered, niggling injuries. The sure-footedness that made him Ireland's best player in the qualifiers for the 1994 World Cup deserted him, and the decline in his confidence was apparent every time he found an opponent's feet with a clearance.

McCarthy stuck by him. Harte was his new man at left-back, but there was always room for his old team-mate in the squad. With a group of young players, experienced heads like Staunton were priceless. He had more than eighty caps, hard as it was to see where the next one was coming from. He went back to Villa and joined the queue for a place in their defence: a spare part for club and country. Then, in May 2001, Gary Breen got injured. He thought he'd be fit enough to play against Portugal, but on the morning of the game he told McCarthy not to risk him. McCarthy went to Staunton, asked him could he do a job at centre-half. McCarthy didn't even have to ask.

For half an hour all the fears about him being too old, too slow, too one-footed were borne out. Luis Figo and Rui Costa skipped unmolested through the Irish defence and Staunton, in particular, looked baffled by the exquisite geometry of their passing. He sliced one clearance that landed, fortuitously, in the hands of Shay Given, while the Portuguese continued to take target practice on the Irish goal for most of the first-half. But they didn't score.

Not unusually for McCarthy's team, they came out after the interval looking like a different group of players. Roy Keane was immense, haring all over the field and scoring the goal that convinced Portugal that a point wasn't so bad after all. A bullet header by Figo gave them that, but Staunton was Ireland's second-best player on the pitch in the second-half, his old tactical mind marshalling the defence brilliantly.

The injury epidemic passed. Centre-halves got well again, but Staunton stayed where he was. McCarthy knew he'd stumbled on something. He had his faults, like all players, but he was Ireland's cleverest defender. McCarthy trusted him. It meant everything to Staunton.

Confidence in him has grown slowly, in increments, as he edges closer to the one hundredth cap that few people ever thought he'd earn. He loves the fact that he was right and they were wrong.

'You boys are very critical of me playing at centre-back,' he says. 'It's just a question of how people perceive you. People just think of me as a left-back, forgetting that I played all of my football in my youth as a centre-back. I played there at Villa under Ron Atkinson, next to Paul McGrath. I've played loads of times as part of a three-man central defence. I really think you lot make a meal of it.'

You lot.

IN MARCH 2001, just before Ireland played in Cyprus, Roy Keane was asked what it meant to him to be winning his fiftieth international cap. It was an invitation to mouth off a few sound bites about what an honour it was to play for his country.

'Absolutely nothing,' he said. There shouldn't have been too much surprise at his reply. He's no sentimentalist. His medals are in a bank vault. The walls of his home are free of anything that might be construed as self-congratulatory. And his Irish caps? It's unlikely he has a room for them.

'I'm not saying that I don't love playing for Ireland. I'm just saying the fiftieth cap isn't different to the rest. It's a game. Maybe without injuries and,' he can't help himself grinning, 'communications problems, we'd have been past that a while ago. There'd be a little more.'

In Cyprus, Keane continued sounding the same note as he had in Amsterdam. The volume got louder, though. 'We've had some decent performances over the years,' he said, 'but things like the Macedonia game, you know, when we could have qualified for a major tournament ... We have to win this kind of match if we want to try and get to Japan.'

And if the players didn't know where he was coming from before, they did now. Every one of them, to a man, left the pitch after the Cyprus game with a dressing-down ringing in his ears. Ireland played badly and won 4-0. Keane provided two of the goals and all of the inspiration. Without him a scoreless draw would not have been inconceivable. In setting a higher standard for himself, he set one for the team too.

'He drove us all on,' Kenny Cunningham said afterwards. 'He shouts and encourages and he's right. When you see the work he does, and then he pops up and scores two goals as well.'

McCarthy didn't stint on his praise of him either. 'Immense,' he said. A couple of days later, he asked in wonder: 'What must it be like to be told you're marking Roy Keane?'

Before the team decamped to Barcelona for the match against Andorra four days later, Keane delivered his prognosis of where the team was now. 'We're not up there with the top nations, but we're getting there. I don't think we would have made the errors we made against Cyprus against better teams.

It's concentration against better teams that counts. That's what wins football matches.'

Following on from his comments about the team's flight arrangements and training facilities, Keane seemed to be talking with the authority of a boss. But at least he and McCarthy seemed to be on the same side.

IS IT TRUE? Could it really be that eight summers have passed since the World Cup in America? Eight years since Ray Houghton's audacious lob and feeble somersault at Giants Stadium. Since Paul McGrath came up against Baggio and Donadoni and gave them not so much as a sniff. Eight summers since Andy Townsend took a bottle of bleach to his hair and the self-styled three amigos, like young Beatles, infected a nation's mood with their insouciance and humour. There was the time they turned up at a press conference wearing wigs. And the time Jason McAteer interrupted an interview with an Australian television station to ask the anchor what was happening in 'Neighbours'. Happy days. Happy, giddy days.

Teenage girls don't lay siege to the Irish team's hotel anymore. They don't scream in McAteer's face, or faint at his feet, or sidle up to him with the intention of asking for an autograph, then find themselves unable to speak and just stare at him instead in a way he always found deeply unsettling. The groupies slipped off once the success did. The hysteria found new objects: Ronan Keatings and Jason Sherlocks. Life went on. McAteer will be thirty-one on his next birthday. He's a father now. A suppressed smile twitches his lips as he considers the implications of being 'one of the Andy Townsend figures' in the squad.

Fame, he discovered, is like a bucking bronco ride. The longer you stay on, the easier it is to convince yourself that you are in control, that you can ride the beast on your terms. But you're kidding yourself. Its movements are utterly unpredictable. One minute you feel like you're in control, your vestibular senses attuned to every bump and jerk it makes. And then, one arbitrary lurch later, you're on your backside, prey to the same gravitational forces as everyone else.

Being let go by Liverpool was like discovering that the love of his life was untrue. He talks about it in short, abbreviated sentences, scared that if he starts speaking his mind he won't stop. But the hurt and bitterness is seldom far from the surface. Packing his bags for relegation-doomed Blackburn was the first sign of sobriety impinging on his world. It's not only age and fatherhood that have knocked the manic edges off McAteer's personality.

'Football is a job to me now,' he says.

Maybe he should have understood better than most the ephemeral nature of it all, because for him the good times came along just as unexpectedly as they departed. He grew up on Merseyside, in Birkenhead, Tranmere Rovers country, but spent his childhood daydreaming of playing for Liverpool alongside Kenny Dalglish, his idol. But football didn't want him.

'Had trials with Tranmere, Chester, Man. United,' he says, 'but I was a small kid, a late developer in height and build, and I slipped through the net. Then you come to that point when you're sixteen years old and you have to decide what you're going to do with your life.'

The imperative was even greater growing up in Liverpool in the depressed 1980s. His father worked as an electrician in the shipyards, the spectre of unemployment forever hanging over the family.

'A ship would arrive in and everything would be great. He'd work for maybe eight months of the year and then get laid-off for the next four. Then they'd pull in another ship and you were back again.'

An A in O-Level art nudged him towards a course in graphic design. 'I did three years in college, but to do well in that game you've got to have a flair. In pretty much everything I've ever done, even football, I'm a worker rather than someone who's naturally gifted. There were people in there coming up with idea after idea, throwing them down on paper. I'd be up all night trying to come up with one.'

So at twenty he was pulling pints in the Sports-man's Arms near Prenton Park and playing non-league football for Marine. He went to America to try out for a scholarship, spent three months in Anapolis, near Washington DC, playing trials matches and secured a place at a university in Chicago. He only came home to tie up some loose ends.

'I played in a reserve team match for Marine against Bolton, and I had one of those unworldly games. Next thing, Phil Neal's ringing me house and asking me down for a week's trial.'

A week later, McAteer was a professional foot-baller. A starring role in Bolton's FA Cup run in 1994 presented him with the choice of an England B cap or a full Irish international one. He had grown up with no sense of his Irish identity, no affiliation with the country. His mother was Welsh, his father English, but his grandfather on his dad's side was born in County Down, a few years before the island was partitioned, which meant he qualified to play for Northern Ireland, or the Republic.

'I didn't choose Ireland just because they'd quali-fied for the World Cup and England hadn't,' he says. 'I was never expected to make the squad for the finals. All I was interested in was going over to Dublin to meet John Aldridge and Ray Houghton and Ronnie Whelan, my heroes because Liverpool was my team, maybe getting to know them and then going to America as a fan to watch them play. That was going to be me summer holidays.'

But in the three friendly matches before the World Cup he skipped exuberantly up and down the right wing and played his way into the squad. The next thing he knew he was nutmegging Paolo Madlini at Giants Stadium.

'The World Cup was like Christmas Day when you're a kid. You get up and suddenly you're wondering where the day's gone. The whole experience was over just like that.'

In another sense it was only beginning. For McAteer, Phil Babb and Gary Kelly new horizons opened. There were modelling assignments, commercials, personal appearances, movie premieres, everything they did accompanied by a soundtrack of shrill female screams and a firewall of minders to keep the madness at one remove.

'The closest thing to it that I have seen is the David Beckham scenario now. We went to Cork to open a shopping centre, thinking maybe fifty or sixty people would turn up. There were thousands. There were girls fainting, getting carried out of the place.

Mick McCarthy with Jack
Charlton. Their admiration for
one another was clear.

(Photo © Inpho)

McCarthy takes his eye off Toto Schillaci for a rare moment during Ireland's defeat to
Italy at the World Cup in 1990. (Photo © Inpho)

An enforcer in the making
– Roy Keane at the World
Cup in the United States
in 1994. (Photo © Inpho)

Keane and Steve Staunton leave the pitch in Orlando after
Holland knocked Ireland out of USA '94. (Photo © Inpho)

Keane was voted Ireland's Player of the Tournament in 1994. (Photo © Inpho)

Two Keanes: Roy offers Robbie polite congratulations after Ireland took a shock early lead in Amsterdam in September 2000. (Photo © Inpho)

Matt Holland earns Ireland a priceless point in Lisbon, in October 2000, with a trademark shot from outside the box. (Photo © Inpho)

Keane rooms alone and guards his privacy jealously.
But he hates being described as a loner. (Photo © Inpho)

Ireland played poorly in Cyprus in March 2002, but won 4-0, Keane
providing two of the goals and all of the inspiration. (Photo © Inpho)

Gary Kelly plants a kiss on Keane's head after his first goal in Cyprus.

(Photo © Inpho)

For half an hour, Portugal looked likely to run in three or four goals in Dublin in June 2001. Then Keane scored and turned the game upside down.

(Photo © Inpho)

Keane's early challenge on Marc Overmars set the tenor when Holland came to Dublin in September 2001.

(Photo © Inpho)

The tension in McCarthy's relationship with
Keane is apparent after the victory over Holland. (Photo © Inpho)

Keane didn't hang around to celebrate
the win over the Dutch.

(Photo © Inpho)

Record-breaker: Niall Quinn throws himself
headlong at the ball to score his record-breaking
twenty-first goal for Ireland against Cyprus
in Dublin in October 2001. (Photo © Inpho)

McCarthy swots up on Iran, his team's World Cup play-off opponents, in Abu Dhabi.

(Photo © Inpho)

We're there: Robbie Keane, Lee Carsley, Ian Harte and Clinton Morrison celebrate in Tehran after their 2-1 aggregate win over Iran in November 2001. (Photo © Inpho)

The prize: McCarthy said he wanted the team to leave Japan with no regrets.

(Photo © Inpho)

McCarthy has always provided a shoulder for Harte to cry on.

(Photo © Inpho)

We got kicked out of a Take That concert at The Point because we were drawing too much attention to ourselves. I'm doing shampoo and Telecom Éireann commercials, book signings. None of my mates back home in Liverpool believed me that this was going on.'

That summer in America provided the basis for a hundred rumours about McAteer and Keane. The word is that they hated each other. There were only three amigos. Keane was around the same age as McAteer, Babb and Kelly, but was never admitted to the club. Not that he had any desire to be. Keane and McAteer would never seek each other out as friends. In many ways they are the very antithesis of each other. Keane takes himself far too seriously to ever get on with McAteer, while McAteer is too frivolous for Keane's liking. McAteer got the attention, the pop-idol hysteria, the girls throwing themselves at him, while Keane quietly settled for being Ireland's Player of the Tournament.

And so the paths of two working-class lads who had once given up on ever becoming professional footballers suddenly diverged. The serious, driven one became the best player in England. The funny, nonchalant one got intoxicated by his fame. Football's popularity exploded. Premiership players were earning telephone-number salaries and dating models and pop stars. Liverpool paid stg£4.5m for McAteer. He could never have considered that his dream move might be the wrong move, but gifted young players who went to Anfield at vital stages of their development went into decline in the 'win, draw or lose, we're straight on the booze' culture at the club. It was no coincidence that the two players arrested for dancing on a car on Harcourt Street were Babb and Kennedy, and McAteer admits he would have been drinking with them that night had he not been playing for Blackburn.

When Liverpool stopped winning trophies, the lifestyles of the so-called Spice Boys came under the microscope. The fans noticed that Manchester United's Christmas party didn't make the front page of the *News of the World*. On Cup final day in 1996, United preferred demure grey suits to Liverpool's garish white. McAteer's team won all the Best-Dressed awards; Keane's won the league and Cup Double. The explanation is too facile for McAteer.

'What you're talking about is a time when football was starting to become big business and very fashionable. We were young lads and, yes, we were getting invited to parties and the Brit Awards and all that. But the United players were doing exactly the same thing as us, unless they were just really, really good lookalikes I was seeing out.'

Gerard Houllier disagreed with McAteer's assessment that the team was 'on the verge of greatness', and when the new broom got to work at Anfield, McAteer was swept out. Liverpool fans would empathise with his view of himself as primarily a worker, but he's remembered fondly as a player who never hid during games and who visibly hurt when the team lost. It isn't difficult to believe him when he says he bawled like a baby when he left the training ground for the last time.

'That was me back to earth,' he says, relegation with Blackburn a few months later hardly breaking the fall.

He was on the rebound for two years after his rejection by Liverpool. In Brian Kidd he found a sympathetic manager who helped him come to terms with his hurt. But Blackburn went down that season and soon McAteer had a new boss. Graeme Souness was like Keane in many ways, not just as a player but as a man, too: hard as granite and uncompromisingly serious. McAteer helped Blackburn return to the Premiership, but it's not difficult to see why Souness would have had a low tolerance for his take on life. McAteer took little seriously.

'He hasn't a bad bone in him,' says Niall Quinn. 'The banter in the dressing room can be very cruel. There's a kind of humour that we footballers have that can cut you right to the bone. He's not like that. When Jason makes you laugh, he's always the butt of the joke himself.'

He likes to tell stories that portray himself as dumb. One has him locking his keys inside his car in Liverpool. He's trying to think of a way in when a policeman arrives on the scene.

'Go and get me a coat-hanger,' the policeman says. McAteer goes into his apartment and returns with a wooden hanger.

'What the fuck do you expect me to do with that?' the policeman asks.

And McAteer says, 'I thought you were going to use it to smash the window.'

In another, he's in the bank with Neil Ruddock, opening his first deposit account. He finds the application form daunting.

'Employer?' he says. 'What do I put down there?'

'You put down Liverpool Football Club, of course,' says Ruddock.

'Oh right,' says McAteer. 'And what about, Position held within company? Do I put down right-wing, or right-wing-back?'

In reality, McAteer just plays up to the Trigger nickname, but his line in self-deprecating humour made it easy to see him as some brainless himbo. But McCarthy loved him. He loved his high-spiritedness and infectious good humour, which counterbalanced Keane's brooding aloofness.

In his darkest moments, McCarthy was more than a manager to McAteer, he was a friend. Last year, his mother-in-law and father-in-law died within eight weeks of each other. McCarthy telephoned to tell him he was thinking about him. Those thoughts meant so much.

But McCarthy wanted him around for more than just entertaining the troops. To him, McAteer was vastly underrated as a footballer. The 'pretty boy' image and a couple of disastrous efforts to convert him into a wing-back had caused the supporters to forget how good a player he really is. When Kennedy was thrown out of the squad, McCarthy's preference for McAteer over Gary Kelly as his stand-in drew groans from the press. Hadn't he used up all his lives? But McAteer went out and played like a man who knew he owed his manager, and it was one of those nights when, for seventy minutes at least, everything worked in blueprint detail.

'Even my goal was something that we'd worked on. Mick McCarthy said I should cut in a lot more to pick off balls from Niall Quinn's head. It was probably the best game I've played for Ireland, in that I set up Robbie Keane's goal as well.'

A year later – frozen out by Souness at Blackburn,

but commanding a new respect in Ireland – he did it again. Holland were throwing everything at Ireland in the second-half at Lansdowne Road, looking for the winner that would put them, and not Ireland, through to the finals. And the Irish ship, down a crew member in Gary Kelly, was listing sharply. Roy Keane gave the defence some respite by taking the ball and leading a rare guerrilla attack on the other end of the field. The ball was played to Damien Duff, then across the edge of the Dutch box to Steve Finnan, who thought about hitting his cross first time, but turned back inside onto his left foot and found McAteer loitering with intent ten yards out. His half-volley was untouchable.

He set off on his victory run, a look of incredulous speculation on his face: could he really be going back to the World Cup finals? He stopped in front of the East Stand and was engulfed by team-mates. What happened next is instructive. McAteer's eyes looked through a clearing in the mass of bodies for Keane, who was arriving to offer his congratulations. It said much that the man who tends to be on the end of most of Keane's explosive rages during matches wanted his imprimatur more than anyone else's. The two high-fived one another. McAteer's expression said, 'Not bad, eh Roy?' Keane's said, 'Sure isn't that what I've been telling you to do?'

The goal earned McAteer a move out of Blackburn to Sunderland, and a manager who likes him. And now, in 2002, he's back at the World Cup again, almost certainly his last, though it's only when he reminisces about his days as an amigo that he remembers his age. He and Babb, he says, are still 'like brothers', godfathers to one another's children. They were never quite as close to Kelly as they were in the public imagination. Kelly became a father soon after the 1994 World Cup and began carving an identity for himself away from the totem of their fame together.

'Me and Phil, we took a lot longer to settle down,' McAteer says.

But now he is settled, more settled than he ever thought he'd be. Some days he's so at peace with the world that he can see himself going back to Anfield to watch his once-beloved Liverpool again.

'My boy, Harry, he's one year old now, but in a couple of years he's going to be looking at all these videos of me running around in a Liverpool shirt, all the pictures on the wall, and he'll say, "What's all this about?" And even though it would hurt too much to go back now, I know one day I'll say, "Come on, son. I'll take you to where your dad used to work." And when he gets there he'll be in awe, just as I was.'

A MILLION WORDS COULD NEVER CAPTURE the stresses in the relationship between Keane and McCarthy as well as Lorraine O'Sullivan's classic portrait of them shaking hands after the victory over Holland. Their body language lays bare their thoughts about one another. McCarthy is standing a whole arm's length away, as if acknowledging the existence of some force field meant to keep him out. Keane's upper body is half-turned towards McCarthy, his lower body is already moving away. There is no eye contact between them. McCarthy is looking down. Keane is looking away. McCarthy appears deferent, submissive, appreciative. Keane seems cold, detached, grudging.

McCarthy is on his way to a party. Keane is on his way home from work. The names of the four children around who his life revolves are written in Indian ink on the bulge of his upper arm. A Dutch player has taken his jersey as a souvenir. Keane has an orange shirt in his left hand, which he may or may not keep. It's an historic day but, unlike McCarthy, he seems unable to enjoy it. The manager moves on to thank the rest of his players and the captain stomps back to the dressing room.

Why was he in such a hurry? And what was going on behind that inscrutable face?

Niall Quinn throws light on it later. He remembers what happened when the rest of the players returned to the dressing room. 'Everybody was jumping around, shouting and roaring,' he says. 'But Roy is there, with a serious expression on his face, telling one player that he should have passed at some stage during the game instead of dribbling it. He is on a different level when it comes to professionalism. He is a machine. I wouldn't say he frightens me, but I would say he intimidates one or two around the squad.'

THE SAVE HIS BOY MADE from Kevin Phillips last season was, to many Newcastle eyes, the best save they'd ever seen. For Seamus Given, the proud father, it was at least up there with the one he had pulled off for Lifford Celtic against Castlefinn Celtic in the semi-finals of the Donegal-area FAI Junior Cup. He was fourteen then.

'They were leading one-nothing with five or six minutes to go and this kid – well, he was like a Craig Bellamy of junior football in Donegal – he struck this shot from thirty-five yards and Shay got across and tipped it out from under the bar. Everyone in Castle-finn still talks about that save.'

On the rare occasions when his encyclopaedic memory of his boy's career fails him, he can fall back on the volumes of newspaper reports he has lovingly clipped out and pasted on to the back of his old technical drawing exercises from school, or the ledger in which he has painstakingly logged every match his son has ever played in, complete with ratings out of ten in the margins. He can run his finger up and down these pages and trace the contours of Shay's career: from his forty-six youth team appearances with Celtic to the last extraordinary season, in which his saves kept Newcastle breathing the thin air at the summit of the Premiership for so long, and stopped Iran taking Ireland's place at the World Cup.

Every entry stirs up a story from his memory. Like the day Shay left home. He was a teenager, but he still looked like a child. When he shuts his eyes he can still picture him, wee baby face on him, learning to drive the brand new lawnmower he bought for the family pitch-and-putt course. Seamus didn't want the boy to go to Glasgow on his own, so he decided to drive him there. They all piled into the car – Seamus, his wife Margaret, the boy and John Lee, the greenkeeper who was also chairman of Lifford Celtic – and they headed to Larne and the ferry to Stranraer.

'Hadn't a clue where we were going,' says Seamus. 'I'd never been outside Ireland in a car before.'

Happy days. A couple of years later, there was his début for Blackburn's reserves against a Lancashire district league side.

'Pat Devlin was scouting for Kenny Dalglish at the time and he was there with me. Couldn't find the pitch and the game was on ten minutes when we finally got there. Shay played well, but he let in two soft goals, misjudged the flight of the ball for one. Just nerves. We were leaving Blackburn at seven o'clock the next morning and the youth development officer at the time, he said to Pat, "It's a good job you'd that contract signed last night before the match." And I says, "Look here, he's seventeen years of age now, I guarantee to you now that he'll have a senior Ireland cap by the time he's nineteen." And he did.'

And there was the day three scouts from Galatasaray arrived at his door in Lifford, wanting to take the boy off to Turkey.

'I can see them yet,' he says, 'dressed all in leather, beautiful leather jackets. They'd an interpreter with them. They were offering big money. They had seen him in action and they were very happy with him. A lot better than he was getting at Blackburn at the time. He was here, home for the summer. They wanted him to sign a contract there and then. I just said no, he was too young, and sent them on their way.'

The father plotted the boy's career; a sort of Earl Woods without the flakiness. It was Seamus who oversaw his move to Celtic, then to Blackburn, then on to Newcastle. Shay can be quiet.

'Never first in the queue when everything's been given out,' says Seamus. He hasn't always been quick to stick up for himself either. So for a long time his father did most of his talking for him. 'He's the kind of guy who would undersell himself,' Seamus says. 'He wouldn't think that he would be as good as other keepers. Like he thinks Barthez is a far better goal-keeper than he is and there's no way that's true. I think most people have acknowledged this season that there's no better goalkeeper in the Premiership than Shay.'

The talent, he didn't exactly lick it up off the ground. Seamus was a goalkeeper himself and the Shay Given story has its beginnings in an unex-pected knock on the door during the August bank holiday weekend of 1967, nine years before Shay was born.

'I'd come home from work, I was at my tea,' he says, 'and I looked out the window and I seen a priest, with a neighbour of mine, coming down the steps to the front door. Didn't know the priest from Adam, didn't know who he was. He came in and introduced himself. Said he was Father Dan Doherty from Aranmore Island. They'd arrived to play in the Convoy Cup final, but their goalkeeper was at sea on a fishing boat and with the stormy weather he never got back to play the game.

'So he's arrived up with my neighbour, Liam McGlinchey, who knew that I played a bit of Gaelic, and that I was a good fielder of the ball, and he asked me would I play. I said certainly I'd play except for the fact that the Ban was in force at the time. This was still the 1960s. If you played Gaelic, you weren't allowed to play soccer. So they agreed that they'd smuggle me into the ground in the boot of a car so I wouldn't be seen. Which is what we did. And that same night we beat Derry Celtic 2-1 and I got Man of the Match. My first time ever keeping goal.'

He saw the inside of a lot of car boots as he pursued his double life over the next few years, playing Gaelic football for Tyrone, where he moved for a short while, and starring incognito as a goalkeeper in summer soccer competitions where the prize money was often as high as £5,000. He played for Coleraine for a while, until they decided to introduce training two nights a week. Seamus had no time for such new-fangled ideas. He quit.

'For me,' he says, 'playing football was just for fun.'

Life was a breeze. But then, in 1980, his world was torn asunder. He lost his first wife – Shay's mother, Agnes – to cancer. Shay was just four years old, one of six children between the ages of two and ten that Seamus was left to rear on his own.

'The day of the funeral,' he says, 'they were trying to split us up. Sisters and brothers and that, all very kindly, offering to take a child here, a child there. I wouldn't hear of it. I said no, we stick together.

'I was playing for Gweedore Celtic at the time. I had to leave them. I was sixty miles from here to Gweedore and I had to be out of the house at eight o'clock on a Sunday morning if we'd a match. I couldn't just pack up six wains and put them in the car. So I transferred to White Strand, just outside Rathmullen, which was only thirty miles away.'

The children became part of the fixtures and fittings at the club, six faces lined up behind the goal. Watching his father keep goal made a lasting impression on Shay. Losing his mother at such a young age played a huge part in shaping his personality, too.

'To this day he carries a photograph of her around in his glove bag. At every match. A photograph and a wee bottle of holy water that she gave him years and years ago when he was very young. His faith is very strong.'

Shay doesn't remember ever meeting Packie Bonner as a boy, but he recalls his 'presence' about Donegal, the hushed reverence with which his name was spoken. But Seamus and Packie went back years.

They played with and against each other for various junior soccer sides in Donegal, and Bonner was understudy to Shay's dad on the county team.

'He was about seventeen at the time,' Seamus recalls, 'and I was twenty-eight, maybe twenty-nine. We were always great friends. I remember helping to get him ready before he went off to Celtic himself, years before Shay ever did. Goodness rest him, there was Dickie Duffy, who was secretary of the Donegal League at the time, myself, Davie Cowan, who was a centre-half with Letterkenny Rovers, and another guy here from Lifford who was a centre-forward. And we used to spend a couple of nights a week up there at St Eunan's College in Letterkenny, preparing him for his Glasgow trip, trying to better him in coming off his lines for crosses. That was his weakest point, you see. So we'd spend hours at a time doing that, throwing the ball up in the air and Packie being challenged by the centre-half and the centre-forward. I suppose Shay was five, maybe six at the time, too young to remember Packie.'

The defining moment in Bonner's career played a part in shaping Shay's life, too. Bonner's save from Daniel Timofte's penalty left a deep imprint on his imagination. Shay's memories of Italia '90 are 'half the neighbourhood watching the matches in our sitting room, cars driving around beeping their horns, flags out the windows.' He was fourteen. Seamus had taken him to a few internationals at Lansdowne Road, to see Bonner and McCarthy, McGrath and Aldridge play. A whole motorcade of coaches would leave the town for Dublin when Ireland played. The five-hour drive back to Lifford would have them home at three o'clock in the morning, and Shay would yawn his way through school the following day.

His own talent as a goalkeeper was already the talk of the northwest. 'He was probably eleven when people started to see it. He was playing Gaelic and soccer at the time and he excelled at both of them. But in soccer he was always ahead of his time. When he was eleven, he was playing under-14. When he was twelve, he was playing under-16. When he was thirteen, he was on the Lifford Celtic intermediate team. He was always that bit ahead of everyone else.'

He was quiet but not shy, certainly not on those occasions when there was a chance to be a hero. Michelle, his sister, ran for Lifford Athletic Club. When Shay was twelve, Seamus took the family to Dublin to see her run in Santry, one of those water-marks of Irish childhood. Shay was there to watch. Then one of the athletes on the under-16 relay team turned over on his ankle. Shay volunteered to run the final leg. They couldn't find a pair of spikes to fit him – he was far bigger than most boys his age – so he ran in a pair of basketball boots with big, chunky soles that barely bent. 'He won the race for them,' Seamus says, 'a boy of twelve in his big boots.'

Manchester United were Shay's team, in open defiance of his father who was a Nottingham Forest man. 'His bedroom was covered in United posters, United bedsheets, United everything.' Peter Schmeichal was his hero. Seamus loved Roy Keane. Shay refused to acknowledge his greatness until he left Forest and joined United, when suddenly he became, to his mind, the greatest player in the world.

When the talent scouts came courting, they were told that Shay was saving himself for Manchester United, or Celtic. There was more to it than just bravado. Why settle for less than you think you're worth? Seamus would reason. And as it happened, they both came looking for him. Celtic were first. Liam Brady was the manager. The first time they shook hands, Brady did a double-take when he saw Shay's giant paws. He was invited to train with Celtic while they were on a pre-season tour of Ireland. Afterwards, over a drink in the Burlington Hotel, Brady turned to Seamus and said, 'Mister Given, I think we've got a five-million-pound goalkeeper on our hands.'

It was agreed that Shay would sign for Celtic when he turned sixteen at the end of the summer of 1992. 'Then Alex Ferguson rang. I told him he was going to Celtic. "Send the boy over," he said. "He'll change his mind when he sees our set-up." I said no, we'd shaken hands on it, given Liam our word.'

So they all piled into the car that September and took the ferry to Scotland. It was an adventure. Saying goodbye to the boy tore him up, though.

'That's where Packie came into play. He acted as a father figure to him when I wasn't there. He was still a child. Too young to leave his brothers and sisters. And they were all very close, especially after their mother died. He was the first link in the chain to break, if you like. So Packie would ring me about things. If he thought he was getting homesick, thinking about throwing in the towel maybe, he'd ring me. In the first six months, I had to go over to him twice a month, that's how bad he was. He never left his digs for the first year. Afraid to go out. Glasgow was too big for him.'

On the rare occasions when he comes home now, Seamus can't believe how much older his son seems since the last time he saw him. Newcastle is his home now. Its size is fine and he's a stranger to nobody. Last year, Seamus went to visit him for the weekend, to take in a game. On the Sunday afternoon, they went shopping and he saw something that shocked him to his core.

'We passed by these three fellas – Newcastle fans they were – and for some reason I looked back. And there they were, down on their hands and knees, kissing the ground that he'd just walked on.'

The ups have come with the inevitable downs, the undulating course of his career reflected in Seamus's meticulously kept ledger. The entries in red pen, he points out, are the matches he's played for Ireland. They start early in the book. He was nineteen when he made his international début, his father's prediction proving uncannily true. Seamus's notes show it was Mick McCarthy's first match in charge, against Russia. He owes McCarthy, he feels. He took a chance on Shay that night. He didn't pick him as a favour. But McCarthy had a perfectly good replacement for Bonner in Alan Kelly and he still gave Shay a chance to prove himself. It's been logged. Not in the ledger. Somewhere more important.

The night of the match, Shay couldn't sit still. He sat in the dressing room and pulled on the jersey that had been left on his peg. And when he pulled his head through it, he looked around him. Paul McGrath was sat on one side of him. Roy Keane was sat on the other. How he loved telling his dad that.

FINAL MELTDOWN TAKES EXACTLY NINE DAYS. The process begins with another of Keane's no-shows and, once again, a communication breakdown that leaves him looking like a selfish, insensitive individual who considers himself bigger than the team. It ends eight time zones away on a remote holiday island in the middle of the Pacific, where all the resentments that have been incubating for ten years finally hatch, where the seething contempt that prevented Keane from meeting McCarthy's eyes finally finds its voice, where the manager hears, in front of twenty-two players who respect him, just how his captain sees him in words that are short and easy to understand.

It starts on Tuesday, 14 May 2002. It's Niall Quinn's big night. Ireland play Sunderland at the Stadium of Light in a benefit match that will raise stg£1m for children's charities in his home town and in his adopted one. Keane doesn't show up. Injury is the explanation. Nothing grave enough to put him out of the World Cup, just an accumulation of wear-and-tear problems with his knee, hip and back that need to be looked after. The engine is older now, it needs constant tuning.

Keane had telephoned Mick Byrne to ask him to pass on his apologies. By any reckoning it is an extraordinary arrangement. Sven Goran Eriksson and David Beckham are enjoying regular meetings and thrice-weekly telephone calls to discuss England's plans for the finals, while the Irish manager and captain are still talking to each other through a third party. Hindsight will tell them that relationships in which there is no communication are doomed to failure. But there is nobody to knock their heads together, so they go on saying what little they have to say to each other through the assistant physio.

McCarthy says he knew Keane wasn't coming, but didn't let on before the game in case it detracted from Quinn's night, perhaps even harmed ticket sales. The explanation is greeted with scepticism by the press. They've been here before. He always has an excuse these days for Keane showing up late, or not showing up at all. The real reason, they suspect, is that it just wasn't Keane's scene. He doesn't *do* testimonials. The truth lies somewhere in between. Keane is at the cinema with his wife, Theresa. He has been away from his family, receiving treatment in France for his injuries, and wants to spend his last night in England with them.

McCarthy's failure to mention it before the match leaves a residue of doubt in the air. There's the player's history. There's *their* history. Keane is about to spend four weeks in the company of a manager he can barely bring himself to look at, with players he refuses to let himself get close to and the press have their antennae attuned to any sign of the old antipathies rubbing bare. In the following day's editions, it goes down as a snub. By the end of the month no one will remember the result of the match in Sunderland, only its place in the chain of events that led to Ireland losing its best player on the eve of the World Cup. And Wednesday's papers will be the first bit of kindling for the fire.

Keane catches a flight to Dublin on Wednesday afternoon. He is given a copy of the *Evening Herald*. The newspaper has consistently refused to accept the line that there is no animosity between Keane and McCarthy, or that Keane has developed a begrudging respect for the manager. In a strongly worded opinion column, Paul Hyland asks why Keane couldn't have put on a shirt and tie and sat in the stand for the night as a show of support for a player he's known for more than ten years. If Keane is angry, it doesn't show when he arrives at the team hotel halfway through dinner. He looks fresh and untroubled and genuinely happy to see the other players. His smile is reciprocated.

He talks to Quinn. There's something he wants to clear up. He turned down the request to write a column for the testimonial programme and he wants to explain his reasons. Cathal Dervan was the journalist who was going to ghost-write it. There is a history of bad blood between them dating back to the day in 1996 when Keane was booed. It was Dervan, writing in *The Title*, who urged Irish supporters to 'let him know what you think' of his no-shows before the match against Iceland. Keane blames him for the booing he received. Dervan and McCarthy, as it happens, are close friends. Dervan is helping McCarthy to write his World Cup diary. McCarthy turned up in court as a character witness in a libel case that Dervan took against Eamon Dunphy. Dunphy is Keane's biographer. The divisions between McCarthy and Keane run a lot deeper than a simple clash of personalities.

Quinn says he understands his reasons and they shake hands. Keane senses a mood of resentment among a number of players towards him. Nobody mentions the match in Sunderland to him. They wouldn't dare. Whether they're annoyed with him or not isn't important. What's important is that Keane feels there's an air of complicity against him. He tells himself that it's going to be a long month.

The following day, Ireland play Nigeria at Lansdowne Road. The match is an awakening for them. They lose 2-1. Out on the pitch, Keane seems crankier than usual. Something is irritating him.

They leave for the World Cup the following morning. There is bedlam in the airport, the players accosted for autographs and bits of conversation in the queue for check-in. Negotiating their way through the departures gate is a stressful, time-consuming operation. In a scene that might have had the unseen hand of Alan Bleasdale directing it, a man dressed in a leprechaun costume puts his arm around a very wound-up Keane and tells him to cheer up. Keane somehow resists the urge to decapitate him.

During the marathon seventeen-hour trip to the team's training base on the island of Saipan, Keane can bite his lip no longer. He launches separate attacks on four journalists, calling them 'scum' for their negative coverage of his non-appearance on Tuesday night. The journey, via Amsterdam and Tokyo, is long and exhausting. During a stop-over in Tokyo, the team are herded into an executive lounge, where Shay Given and Damien Duff decide that the atmosphere needs lightening. They put on *Gift 2*, a CD of Today FM breakfast show sketches, and skip forward to the 'Candid Camera Roy' sketch, in which a bank-teller in Cork tells him that his account is in the red. 'All credit *to* debit, but I'd like to make a simple withdrawal, *at* the end of the day.' They succeed where the leprechaun failed. Keane is caught chuckling to himself in a corner.

Saipan is still three hours away. The island has been chosen by McCarthy for a week of rest and acclimatisation in the searing, thirty-five-degree heat. Finally they arrive at their destination. Walking through the baggage hall, the players are each handed a Hawaiian-style garland of flowers. Jason McAteer puts his on his head. So does McCarthy. So do Duff and Given. Nobody notices what Keane does with his, but he's not wearing it. His expression says: here on business. The players receive a short history lesson. Saipan, they're told, was captured by US troops as they island-hopped their way across the Pacific in the last months of the Second World War. It was from here that they launched the two atomic bomb attacks on Japan, which brought the war to an end. In the days ahead, the history books will be ransacked for metaphors to describe the new war that's building up.

On Sunday, Keane gets his first sight of the pitch where the players will train for a week before moving on to Japan. All the bad vibes he's had about this trip from the moment he arrived in Dublin are justified. The pitch is bone-hard and full of craters. What's more, the footballs and training kit aren't waiting for them at the ground. The players are forced to do a training session without footballs and in their casual-wear. They shake their heads and say it's typical of the FAI. McCarthy apologises. The joke on the bus is that they feel like they're playing for a pub team.

They all come up with different names. The Pig and Whistle. The Dog and Duck. The Horse and Hound. Most of them laugh about it and move on. Keane doesn't. He's seething. He can't see the rainbow for the rain.

The players return to the Hyatt Hotel. A barbecue that night offers the players the chance to get to know the Irish journalists who'll be covering the World Cup, an idea Keane regards with utter revulsion. To take part, he feels, would make him a hypocrite. To stay away, though, would give credence to the popular image of him as some cranky loner. So he goes. He spends an hour or two talking to Mick Byrne and Alan Kelly, then makes his excuses and returns to his room. The party repairs to the Beefeater Pub across the road. The players return at five o'clock in the morning. They've had a good night. Maybe Keane hears them.

On Monday morning the players sleep off whatever damage they did to themselves the night before. Training is scheduled for the afternoon. By now Keane has settled into what will become a routine for him while he is on the island. When he isn't training he is walking off his energy on the nearby beach, he's sitting in his room, reading, or he's in the hotel gym, lifting weights. Training goes ahead in the afternoon. The skips containing the equipment still haven't arrived. It's all a bit Irish. Keane doesn't see the joke. They are on the way to the World Cup. The first match against Cameroon is less than a fortnight away. He wonders is he the only one taking it seriously. He has worked hard for this. Made sacrifices. He has spent weeks away from his wife and children. And what has he been saying for the past two years? *We've got to start giving ourselves a bit more credit. We have good players. You get a bit sick and tired of the whole, "well, the Irish will have a good time no matter what the result" stuff.* Was nobody listening?

He knocks on McCarthy's door that night and tells him that, as captain, he's unhappy with the lack of rigour that's going into the preparations. McCarthy says he's just as annoyed as Keane is about the skips and the state of the pitch.

'But you have to hold your hands up,' Keane tells him. 'You're the manager. The buck stops with you.'

McCarthy says that promises were made and were not kept.

'You can't rely on promises when the World Cup is at stake,' Keane replies

McCarthy reminds him that the week in Saipan was never supposed to be about rigorous training. It was about resting up after a long season and adjusting to the heat and the time difference. It's a scene laden with irony. Ten years after questioning Keane's professionalism on the team bus in Boston, McCarthy is listening to a homily on the subject from the same man. Keane is not happy when he leaves.

On Tuesday, Kevin Kilbane talks to a television reporter about the inevitable friction that occurs when twenty-three grown men are corralled together in the same hotel for four weeks on end. Over the course of the World Cup, he says, there is bound to be 'an argument or two'. He gets the numbers eerily right.

The first pre-tremors are felt at training. There's tetchiness in the sweaty air. Gary Kelly and Packie Bonner, the goalkeeping coach, exchange sharp words. So do Lee Carsley and David Connolly. At the end of training, the three goalkeepers – Shay Given, Alan Kelly and Dean Kiely – take sanctuary from the sun in the shelter beside the pitch. Keane asks Ian Evans where they're going. The practice match is about to start. Evans tells him that Bonner had them out half an hour earlier than usual. 'They're knackered, Roy.'

Keane says, 'We're all knackered. Isn't that what we're here for?'

The match goes ahead without goalkeepers. They play 'nearest to the goal'. As usual, Keane plays as if every tackle matters. After the match he makes a beeline for Bonner.

'Why were the goalies not playing?' he asks.

Bonner explains quietly that they had started their drills half an hour early and were tired.

'Tired?' Keane says. 'You won't be too tired to play golf tomorrow, will you?' He throws his water bottle on the ground in a fit of temper. Bonner looks around him, like he can't believe Keane is behaving like this in front of an audience. Alan Kelly, the nearest Keane has to a friend in the squad, says, 'Will you calm down, Roy.' Keane shouts, 'Are you going to make me calm down?' The reaction of the other players is interesting. They seem not to be watching. They sit with their water bottles, staring impotently into the middle distance, too shocked to say anything and at the same time wishing it away. Keane stomps off. When the other players get on the bus, he is there before them, sitting alone, staring at the ceiling.

Five minutes after they return to the hotel, Keane is back at McCarthy's door. He tells him he's going home. It's not a fit of pique. It's not an act of brinkmanship. He means it. He even has the presence of mind to say, 'It's not too late for you to call someone else up.' McCarthy asks him, 'Is it me, Roy?' Keane says no. McCarthy asks, 'Is it the training ground, then?' Keane says no. McCarthy asks, 'Is it the flight? The airport?' Keane says, 'No, it's me. It's personal.'

Phone calls are made and a flight off the island is booked in Keane's name. A replacement set of gear is ordered with the name of Colin Healy, the young Celtic midfielder, on the back and – the bombshell – the number six underneath. Word spreads like a susurration through the rest of the squad. In his diary in the *Sunday Independent*, McAteer tells how he goes to Keane's room to check whether everything's okay. Keane is brushing his teeth. 'Not really,' he says.

'Come on, we've got to get on with it now,' McAteer says. Keane just smirks at him. 'You're not really going home, are you?'

'Four o'clock tomorrow.'

'Good one.'

'We'll see.'

McAteer returns to his room where Steve Staunton is sleeping in the other bed. He tells him the news. Staunton is confused, then angry. He gets up and goes to find Quinn.

The official reason offered for Keane's departure is the long-standing problem with his knee and some unspecified 'personal worries'.

Back in Dublin, the FAI react to the news with utter disbelief. Treasurer John Delaney telephones Keane's solicitor, Michael Kennedy, whom he knows from their discussions over the players' pool, and asks

126

if the situation is retrievable. Kennedy says he'll talk to Keane and to other people he's likely to listen to, including his wife and the Manchester United manager Alex Ferguson. In the meantime, Delaney says, he'll speak with Liam Gaskin, McCarthy's agent, and with McCarthy himself.

Keane wakes up at 6.30am, determined that he's going home today. He telephones Theresa and she tells him that Kennedy has rung, desperate to talk to him. Ferguson wants to speak to him as well. He returns both calls. It's Ferguson who changes his mind, telling him to think about his family in Cork and what they would be forced to endure if he were seen to desert the squad on the eve of the World Cup. It takes a few hours, but eventually Keane is coaxed back down from the edge. Persuading McCarthy to take him back is more difficult, but he too relents. Healy gets a phone call apologising for the trouble and a fax is sent to FIFA, correcting an earlier squad list that had Keane's name omitted. It makes the deadline with five minutes to spare. There is peace. But the only thing that McCarthy and Keane have in common as they begin a new day, drained from lack of sleep, is the uneasy sense that it's not going to last.

On Wednesday morning, Keane's mood hasn't improved. McAteer meets him in the treatment room.

'You all just go with the flow,' Keane says to him.

'What do you mean?' McAteer asks.

'What goes with the flow?' Keane says.

'I don't know.'

'Dead fish,' he says and then walks out.

A team meeting is called for nine o'clock. Again, McCarthy apologises for the kit going missing and for the condition of the pitch, but repeats that the serious work is not due to start until Friday, when they move to Izumo, their training base in the west of Japan. At training that day, Alan Kelly makes light of what happened the day before by turning up in a balaclava. Keane appreciates gallows humour and gets a good laugh out of it.

After training they return to the hotel. Half of the squad go to play their much-derided round of golf. The rest go to the cinema to watch *Attack of the Clones*. Keane does neither. He stays at the hotel and does two interviews, one with Paul Kimmage of the *Sunday Independent*, the other with Tom Humphries of *The Irish Times*, two of only a handful of journalists he trusts.

He is clearly unhappy with his decision to stay and there are still a number of resentments festering. Over the next couple of hours he unburdens himself of quite a lot. What he says is explosive. He feels like he's been banging his head off the wall by

Keane meets Taoiseach Bertie Ahern at Dublin Airport on the way to the World Cup 2002. Keane already had bad vibes about the trip. (Photo © Inpho)

Keane throws a water bottle at the end of a furious row with goalkeeping coach Packie Bonner in Saipan. (Photo © Inpho)

Going their separate ways: McCarthy and Keane, just hours
away from the inevitable end. (Photo © Inpho)

Keane cuts a lonely figure as he makes his way home from Saipan. (Photo © Inpho)

Alan Kelly, Niall Quinn, Mick McCarthy, FAI President Milo Corcoran and Steve Staunton face the media to explain why Keane was sent home.

(Photo © Inpho)

Keane's expulsion dominated the front pages back home.

(Photo © Inpho)

McCarthy tells his players that there is life after Keane.

(Photo © Inpho)

Matt Holland puts in a Keane-style tackle on Cameroon's
Pierre Wome in Ireland's opening match in Niigata. (Photo © Inpho)

Shay Given retrieves the ball while Gary Kelly wonders if there's any way
back after Patrick Mboma put Cameroon into the lead. (Photo © Inpho)

A disbelieving Matt Holland is mobbed by Mark Kinsella, Robbie Keane, Kevin Kilbane and Damien Duff after his equaliser against Cameroon.

(Photo © Inpho)

Robbie Keane scores the dramatic, last-gasp equaliser against Germany in Ibaraki. (Photo © Inpho)

With the cartwheel he started performing at Crumlin United, Keane celebrates the goal that kept Ireland in the World Cup.

(Photo © Inpho)

Robbie Keane owed McCarthy a greater debt for his loyalty
than most players. (Photo © Inpho)

Robbie Keane volleys the first of Ireland's three goals
against Saudi Arabia in Yokohama. (Photo © Inpho)

Damien Duff runs rings around
Saudi Arabia's Mohamed Al-Jahani.

(Photo © Inpho)

McCarthy celebrates with
his backroom staff after
Ireland secure their
passage into the second
round. (Photo © Inpho)

McCarthy arrives in Seoul,
South Korea, insisting that
Ireland need have no fear of
Spain. (Photo © Inpho)

Carlos Puyol climbs high above Kevin
Kilbane to foil another Irish attack.

(Photo © Inpho)

The end: McCarthy thanks Quinn for
all the years he gave him.

(Photo © Inpho)

Kevin Kilbane, Damien Duff, David Connolly and Kenny Cunningham watch grimly as
Ireland exit the World Cup on penalties. (Photo © Inpho)

complaining about the training camp. The kit should have been on the island two weeks before the team arrived, he says, to ensure it was there for them. The pitch is harder than the hotel car park and two players have already injured themselves on it.

'[But] we're the Irish team,' he says. 'It's a laugh and a joke. We shouldn't expect too much.'

What makes it worse is that they travelled seventeen hours to the other side of the world for these facilities. The World Cup is ten days away, he says, they shouldn't have to think about these things.

'Playing Cameroon next Saturday, it's going to be so bloody hard. We could be in for a shock.'

Again, when he speaks, it's as though he's assuming the role of the boss. 'If wanting the best is a crime, then I'm guilty ... At Manchester United they want the best of everything. That's the difference. They want it. Everybody. When we travel, the treatment is fantastic because of that. People in the laundrette, the canteen, feel that way at United.' He will quit international football after the World Cup. 'Enough is enough,' is his mantra. In the meantime, he will put his head down and do his best for 'myself, the people of Ireland and my family. Sod everybody else.'

When the players arrive for training the following morning, the first copies of *The Irish Times* are running off the presses in Dublin. Just after lunch, McCarthy is reading a transcript of the interview, which has been printed off the internet. What he reads infuriates him. Keane, he feels, has twisted their differences to make it sound like a contest between his sense of professionalism and McCarthy's. Soon it's the talk of the players. For them, one quote screams off the page: 'All the players feel the same. They react differently. Some people accept it easier. Maybe that's why they're playing where they are.' For years they have wondered what Keane, in his private thoughts, really felt about them. Now they have their answer.

'He thinks we're shit,' Jason McAteer tells Paul Kimmage.

The strained atmosphere over dinner that night is a forewarning of what's coming. McCarthy wants to see the full squad and the technical staff at 7.30pm, ostensibly to clear the air. Only Keane and McCarthy are aware of the *realpolitik* of the meeting. McCarthy wants to force a conclusion and Keane wants it as well. The way they've been behaving around one another for the past few years is foreign to both of them. They are two fundamentally decent men who look for warmth and honesty and loyalty and respect in their relationships. There has never been much of that between them. Their relationship has been a contrivance. Hatchets were buried. Issues were parked. Resentments were covered over. Things that needed to be said went unsaid. They held back the tide.

McCarthy indulged Keane, turned a blind eye whenever he reported in a day later than the rest of the players, only to announce that he was too tired to take part in the practice match. McCarthy defended him to the press, even when it looked like his authority was being tested. He acknowledged that he was one of the greatest players in the world and, in return, Keane refrained from saying what he really thought of his manager. It worked for them. What Keane brought to the team couldn't be ignored. The younger players McCarthy was trying to fashion into a team worshipped Keane. And while he offered them only tough love in return, he taught them to believe in themselves, to walk tall, shoulders back, chin up. He told them they were good enough to go to the World Cup. He told them not to be happy just to draw with the best teams in the world. He told them not to smile meekly at the blazers in the first-class cabin before squeezing themselves into their economy-class seats. He offered them little insights into the way things were done at Manchester United. There was friction between captain and manager, but the players buzzed off the energy. And when they played, they wanted to please them both. But it couldn't last. There could be only one gaffer.

McCarthy can't be unaware of what Keane's likely reaction will be when he arrives at the team meeting with a copy of *The Irish Times* interview and invites him to air any grievances he has in front of the team and the technical staff.

'Who the fuck do you think you are having meetings about me?' Keane asks.

The exchanges come thick and fast. McCarthy reminds him of how he's been pampered. 'You give people hell,' he tells him. 'You pick and choose your games.'

Keane demands to know what McCarthy means and Ireland's final qualifier in Iran is mentioned. Keane had just returned from injury, was facing a long season and had to be more sparing on his body. They cut a deal. Keane would play in the first leg in Dublin. If McCarthy felt the job was done, he wouldn't be asked to travel to Tehran. Ireland won the first leg 2-0 and Keane returned to Old Trafford, as it happens without saying goodbye or good luck to his team-mates. McCarthy would later deny accusing him of feigning injury, but Keane flies into a temper and what's been eating him all these years comes out in an unstoppable torrent. He is 'white with rage' according to one player. Most of the players are too shocked to remember the exact detail of everything that was said, but the highlights make the following day's papers.

'You were a crap player and you're a crap manager,' he tells him. 'The only reason I've any dealings with you is that somehow you are the manager of my country.' There will be some debate later about whether Keane made an issue of McCarthy's 'Englishness' during the tirade. He will deny claims that he did. But McCarthy says, 'If you don't have any respect for me, then don't play for me.' Keane calls him a 'fucking wanker'.

'Stick it up your bollocks,' is his postscript to their relationship.

When he leaves the room, Gary Kelly asks, 'Is that it then? Is it really over?'

McCarthy tells the players, 'We go on from here now. We'll grow stronger from this. We stick together.'

Kiely, the substitute goalkeeper, raises his hand. He's normally a quiet character, although fiercely independent. Three years ago, in the European Championships play-off in Turkey, he responded to a dressing-down from Keane by giving him one back. It gives him a certain cachet within the squad. 'I just want you to know,' he tells McCarthy, 'that I can do a job for you in midfield on Saturday.' The tension dissolves into laughter. McCarthy departs to tell Keane that he's sending him home, but Keane doesn't need to be told it's over.

A press conference is called to announce the news. McCarthy is flanked by Staunton, Kelly and Quinn, his three most senior players offering support for his stance. 'As a player of his stature, I'm very sad to lose him,' McCarthy says. 'Absolutely. But as a squad member, I'm not bothered one bit that he's gone. This action has been taken and all twenty-three of the players were there when it happened. It was a very public, very open show of opinions and hostility.

'I was tired of standing up for people, supporting people. And all I would like is to be treated the way I treat people. I wanted it reciprocated and it wasn't. So I've no worries about what is happening ... Those comments in the newspaper are all well and good, but I don't see many complaints from anyone else. Sometimes Roy sees the world through his own eyes, completely different to everyone else.'

Staunton, who has agreed to replace Keane as captain, says: 'It was unacceptable ... There is a line. You can't cross it. And unfortunately, Roy has crossed it.'

Kelly adds, 'Roy has let himself down with the things he said. I've never witnessed anything like it.'

The team moves on to Izumo in Japan the following day. McCarthy says he wants no mention of

Keane once they leave the island. He doesn't want to feel the weight of his shadow cast over the World Cup. It's a forlorn hope. 'No one man is bigger than the team,' McCarthy says, and seldom has it sounded so empty and clichéd.

JUST BEFORE EIGHT O'CLOCK ON SATURDAY NIGHT, there's a sharp knock on Niall Quinn's door. It's David Connolly. He looks wretched: drawn and troubled. He says he needs to talk and Quinn invites him in. Ireland have just scraped a 2-1 win out of a match against Sanfreece Hiroshima, a mid-table Japanese league side. A week shy of the World Cup, the priority was for the players to get through the match without doing any damage to themselves, but even allowing for that, Ireland's performance was insipid, flat, the players looking jaded by what had happened during the past few days.

To crown a week in which all the fun was wrung out of their World Cup adventure, Jason McAteer returned to the hotel with his knee swathed in bandages. A tackle that would have been construed as an assault had it not happened within the confines of a football pitch put him in doubt for Ireland's first match.

Connolly sits on the bed and gets straight to the point: he wants Roy Keane back. He's asked around and he isn't the only one who feels that way. For Quinn, the words are exciting. For two nights he's lain awake, thinking over all the things he could have done to stop events taking the turn they did. What if he'd interrupted Keane when he'd started raging at McCarthy? Why didn't he say something, anything, just to deflect the flame-thrower of Keane's anger away from McCarthy and onto himself? Why didn't he say something funny to release the tension from the moment. But he said nothing. Just sat there, like the rest, eyes agape, jaw unhinged, while everything they'd grafted so hard for was torn apart in front of them. Connolly suggests ringing Michael Kennedy to see if he'd act as a conduit between Keane and McCarthy. Quinn tells Connolly that if there's anything he can do to bring Keane back, he'll do it.

Six hours earlier, at Heathrow Airport, Keane arrives after his long, lonely trip back from Saipan and catches his connection to Manchester. By the time he emerges through the arrivals gate, blinking hard in the glare of a hundred flashbulbs, he has already spoken to his agent. Kennedy has told him that he needs to put his side of the story across, and quickly. Keane isn't bothered. He has said what he had wanted to say. Kennedy tells him it's important. McCarthy is winning the popular vote again, just like he had six years earlier.

Kennedy had thought about issuing a statement to the Press Association, but the cold, stilted language of a press release would not win over the public. They'd been down that road in the summer of 1996. This time he would do an interview. The *Mail on Sunday* had already telephoned. Keane agreed to sit down with Peter Fitton, the newspaper's football correspondent, who is close to Alex Ferguson, and put forward his side of the story, which will be splashed across the front page of the following day's edition.

RTÉ have also been on the case. The previous afternoon Tommie Gorman had called Kennedy's office in London. By some fluke of fate, the publicity-shy agent answered the telephone himself. RTÉ's London correspondent, Brian O'Connell, was on leave and Gorman had been assigned to cover the story. What he wanted, he explained, was the first television interview with Keane. Kennedy told him that Martin Bashir had already been on and wanted the same thing. Gorman reminded him that an interview with RTÉ would reach a wider Irish audience. Kennedy said he'd get back to him.

Undeterred, Gorman flies from London to Manchester and hangs around outside Keane's house. Kennedy checks Gorman's *bona fides* with Eamon Dunphy, who tells him of his reputation as a tough and respected journalist, and is assured that the interview would reach a prime-time audience. At 10.30am on Monday, Kennedy telephones Gorman's mobile phone to tell him he's got the scoop of the year. Gorman books a room at the Moat House Hotel in Manchester.

When Connolly leaves his room, Quinn thinks long and hard about what to do next. He picks up the telephone and calls Kennedy. The two go back years. It was Quinn who introduced Kennedy to Keane, his most famous client, and to Connolly, who became the highest-paid player in Dutch football because of Kennedy's skills as a negotiator. They speak for half an hour. Quinn tells him that some of the players want Keane back. Kennedy asks him what McCarthy wants and Quinn says that McCarthy doesn't know he's ringing. Keane is still livid, Kennedy says, over his treatment not just by McCarthy, who he feels set him up at the player meeting, but also by the FAI, which stood by while he made his own arrangements to go home. Talking Keane down would be difficult, he says, but he'll try. In the meantime, he warns him, Keane has given an interview to the *Mail on Sunday* in which he has criticised his old team-mates, especially Quinn, Staunton and Alan Kelly. Ignore whatever he said, Kennedy tells Quinn. He just needed to let off steam.

Dean Kiely, Mark Kinsella and Ian Harte are the three players rostered to talk to the press on Sunday afternoon. The daily press conferences have been fraught with tension ever since Keane's departure. All of the players have their own private view of what happened, who was right and who was wrong, and sticking to the agreed script has been difficult at times. But Kiely puts on a virtuoso performance, helping out his two team-mates when they struggle with some of the more awkwardly bouncing questions thrown at them, and repeating the agreed line that there is life in this team after Roy Keane.

'We've come here to work,' he says. 'We didn't book this trip with Thomas Cook.' Keane is no longer an issue, he says, and the players don't even mention his name anymore. But it isn't true.

That morning, McCarthy had travelled by chopper to the city of Kobe to watch Cameroon draw 2-2 with England in their final warm-up match. While he was away, Quinn took the opportunity to sound out the players. Some wanted Keane back. Some didn't. All afternoon he moved from room to room, talking, reasoning, persuading.

'Not every player felt the exact same way at the exact same time,' says Quinn. 'Some people welcomed it immediately. Some people said, "Hang on a minute, he's done this and he's done that."

Eventually, when I got to the end of my efforts, it was unanimously felt that, for the people back home, trying to sort this out was the right thing to do, bearing in mind the circumstances and the furore that was caused and the reaction of the Irish people.'

What Quinn did was extraordinary: its effect was to completely undermine McCarthy's authority. In Jack Charlton's time, it wouldn't have happened. Had Charlton thrown a player out of the team, no one would have dared question his decision, much less start agitating behind his back to bring the player back. But Quinn said he couldn't have lived with himself had he not tried.

Cameroon's performance against England has given McCarthy enough to occupy him without returning to find the Keane business exhumed. When he finds out how Quinn spent his day, he is furious. Once he's calmed down, he gives Quinn the impression that there is still some room for manoeuvre. 'It's going to have to be one hell of an apology,' he says.

In the broad, breezy lobby of the Royal Hotel in Izumo, there are three laptop computers, all with access to the internet. By the time Sunday night segues into Monday morning, even the less computer-literate members of the squad have read the printouts of Keane's *Mail on Sunday* interview, which have been passed around. What he's said is ill at odds with Quinn's claim that Keane and McCarthy's differences could still be smoothened out. Far from being ready to say sorry, Keane said *he* was owed the apology. He accused McCarthy of being out to settle old scores after his put-down of him in America ten years earlier. Most of the players, he said, had agreed with his criticisms of the slipshod arrangements the FAI had made, but were too frightened to speak out. He felt betrayed by the senior players – Quinn, Staunton and Kelly – who could have added weight to his complaints by speaking out.

'Some people are sheep and some are wolves,' he'd said darkly. 'There are a lot of sheep over there and probably I am a wolf.'

Quinn speaks to Kennedy more than a dozen times on Sunday, two men whose sleeping patterns have been knocked so off kilter they're no longer aware that there are eight time zones between them. The interview has done damage, the players are unhappy with the way they've been characterised. Kennedy tells him not to worry. Keane wants to go back to Japan, he is sure of it. The interview with Tommie Gorman has been fixed for the following day, and he is sure that Keane will offer some conciliatory noises that might placate McCarthy. Quinn goes to bed. Sleep comes but in small rations.

Monday is the longest day Quinn ever

remembers. In the morning, he loses an important ally in Ireland's new captain. Staunton comes to his room and tells him that his wife is upset about Keane's newspaper interview and what he said about Staunton and the other senior players. It doesn't feel right, Staunton says, trying to persuade the players that Keane's return was in everyone's best interests. Quinn says he understands. The day drags by, but Quinn is still excited, having convinced himself and most of the other players that Keane is going to apologise to McCarthy on national television tonight.

Quinn is bristling with anticipation. He can't stop checking his watch. He stays up until the early hours. It's close to three o'clock in the morning when he telephones Gillian, his wife. He gets straight to the point: how did the interview go? He mentioned the footballs and the training kit again, she says. And the pitch that was too hard for the players to train on. And how the older players in the squad had left him to fight his own corner at the meeting. 'But did he apologise?' Quinn snaps. Gillian says it was difficult to tell. He sounded reasonable – reachable, even – without expressing any actual words of regret.

Unfortunately, that tone isn't conveyed in the copies of the transcript that McCarthy and the players read over breakfast on Tuesday morning. Stripped of the emotion that was clear on television, Keane appears to be more trenchant than ever. Some sections leap off the page: 'If there was any doubt in my mind that, "Roy, you were a little bit out of order, you should maybe have held it back a little bit," I'd be back like a shot. But I won't accept, I can't accept, this'; 'I went to my room and we had three players at a press conference within half an hour sitting behind Mick. People look at them as role models. They are cowards'; 'I'm sticking to my guns because my gut feeling is that what happened to me last week was wrong. It was wrong. And you can go around the houses and talk about different things, but it was wrong and I wouldn't wish it on anyone'; 'my conscience is clear'.

A gaggle of journalists who have stayed up all night writing about the Keane interview arrive at dawn at the Royal Hotel in a convoy of taxis to get McCarthy's reaction to it. The hotel staff wake Brendan McKenna, the FAI's press officer, who says he knows nothing about the RTÉ interview. It kicks off a day of high farce for the FAI. McCarthy is woken next, but he refuses to give an interview, determined to speak to his players first.

The response to Keane's interview in Ireland is an outpouring of public sympathy, the extent of which is difficult to appreciate from eight thousand miles away. It's clear, though, that in twenty-four hours he has turned the tables on McCarthy, as the manager acknowledges when he finally speaks: 'It's easier to win the public relations battle from a studio in Dublin, when it's just you and the interviewer and the lights, than it is to do it in a press conference situation on the other side of the world.'

As far as McCarthy is concerned, Keane has not budged one millimetre from his position, despite Quinn's promises. If anything, he has dug himself in further. The clues that he might still be turned are too faint, too subtle to see in black and white. Asked whether he would return if the players said they wanted him back, Keane said: 'I really don't know, because I can't see it happening.' Asked whether he saw any way of putting the episode behind him and returning to Japan, he said, 'Maybe. Maybe. But it's out of my hands.'

At 10.30am the players are summoned to another team meeting. McCarthy, hurt by their refusal to accept his final word on Keane, tells them he's leaving it up to them to decide whether to take him back. Some take it as a him-or-me ultimatum. McCarthy steps out of the room and Quinn asks each and every player in turn for his opinion. Everyone speaks, some of them at length. It takes almost an hour for everyone to have his say. At the end of it, there is unanimity. The players decide to stand by their manager's original decision, just as he has stood by them in their troubled times. Any other decision would have made McCarthy's position untenable. Quinn tells him of the decision. McCarthy decides to kill the issue dead at his daily press conference.

The team arrives for training one hour late. McCarthy steps onto the pitch whistling a happy tune. He makes a point of posing for the photographers and quips, 'It kills you lot when I smile.' Something is stirring. It's in the air. Midway through training, Jason McAteer is overheard asking Eddie Corcoran, the FAI's logistics officer, 'Have they got it yet?' *It* is a statement scribbled down by the players on a sheet of hotel notepaper during the ten-minute drive from the hotel to the training ground, expressing their support for their manager and declaring the Keane issue dead and buried.

The statement reads: 'Regrettably, the manner of Roy's behaviour prior to his departure from Saipan, and the comments attributed to him since, have left the staff and players in no doubt that the best interests of the squad are best served without Roy's presence.'

The statement is supposed to be held until after McCarthy's own press announcement that morning that there was no possibility of any comeback for

Keane. But McCarthy postpones his meeting with the media, and the announcement, until later in the day to allow FAI general secretary Brendan Menton to get back from the FIFA congress in Seoul. Somehow the statement by the players, which has been given to McKenna to type, is released to the press. The players climb on the bus and return to their rooms, leaving an out-of-his-depth McKenna to field questions about who was in charge of the team, McCarthy or his players.

'Our fault,' Quinn says later. 'Nobody told Brendan that it wasn't to be released straight away. And so it was, to the horror of us all.'

Despite the declaration of support for McCarthy, Quinn's efforts to get Keane to make a gesture continue. He maintains a three-way telephone contact with Kennedy and John Delaney, the FAI's treasurer, who had helped defuse the first row in Saipan. Between them, they work out a formula of words that Keane could use to express regret at what happened while not losing face. The fudge requires Keane to accept, publicly, that his comments were 'deeply hurtful' to McCarthy and to assert his desire to play in the World Cup. Kennedy believes Keane will agree to the script. Quinn promises to work on McCarthy.

There is another problem. All of the delicate work the three have done to persuade Keane back will unspool once he hears about the players' statement. Quinn tells Kennedy it was a terrible mistake and asks him to assure Keane that it isn't how the players feel.

At teatime on Tuesday, Quinn explains his behind-the-scenes efforts at making peace at an emotionally charged press conference. On his way back to the hotel, he again telephones Kennedy, who tells him that Keane has come round even further. He is prepared to use the agreed words, if he thinks McCarthy will accept them in lieu of an outright apology. When Quinn returns to the hotel he is still upset and he takes the lift to McCarthy's room. The two talk for forty-five minutes, Quinn pleading with the manager to give Keane one more chance. McCarthy agrees. There's no need for any abject apologies, he says. Keane just has to ring him and they'll talk and sort it out. When they're finished talking, Quinn says, they're both in tears.

The word is out that there are three private jets fuelled and waiting to take Keane back to Japan. The Taoiseach Bertie Ahern has made the Government airplane available, JP McManus has offered his jet, as have Manchester United.

McCarthy leaves the hotel for his own press conference at the media centre. It will stick in the memory for two reasons. Firstly, there are Menton's interruptions whenever McCarthy looks like saying anything intemperate about Keane. McCarthy has never looked so undermined in his six years as Ireland manager, his players plotting behind his back to undo the biggest decision he's ever made, while the FAI fail to back him like they would have backed Charlton. Secondly, there is a clear softening in McCarthy's stance after his tearful talk with Quinn. He no longer declares Keane gone for good nor the subject of his return off-bounds. He doesn't believe an apology is something that can be negotiated, he says, but if the players want Keane back, he will abide by their wishes. Either way, it is still going to require a phone call from Keane.

'The wait for Mick McCarthy to do his press conference was an eternity,' Quinn says. 'He came back and told me he felt he hadn't got his point across properly, that it was a bit of a fiasco. But I was delighted when he told me to go ahead, get the message to Michael Kennedy to get Roy to ring him and he can come back. Michael had assured me that he had the offer of three private jets to get him here, and I was convinced he was going to come back. And we spoke hourly after that, probably even more, until one o'clock in the morning Japanese time, when he [Kennedy] asked me, "What has Roy got to do in this phone call?" I said, at this stage all Roy has to do is make it and say to Mick he wants to play in the World

Cup and that last week's actions were wrong, which he'd already said in the newspaper. And Michael felt really confident he'd get this from Roy.'

Kennedy telephones Keane at around five o'clock in the afternoon in Manchester and tells him what's on offer. Alex Ferguson calls and urges him to go back. Keane takes the dog out for a walk and turns it over and over in his mind.

Just after half-past three in the morning, the telephone on Quinn's bedside locker rings. It's Kennedy. Keane has decided not to come.

A statement issued to RTÉ on Keane's behalf thirty minutes later adds a full-stop to the whole business. 'In the interests of all genuine supporters of Irish football,' it reads, 'I believe that the time has now arrived when I should bring a conclusion to the continuing speculation with regard to my participation in the World Cup and for the players to concentrate fully on their preparations for the competition, free from all further distraction.

'Whilst I appreciate all the support which I have received and all the efforts which have been made by a number of people on my behalf of all the parties involved in this unfortunate matter, I do not consider the best interests of Irish football will be served by my returning to the World Cup.

'The damage has been done. I wish the team and

the management all the best and they will have my full support throughout the competition. I urge all the people of Ireland to give their entire support to the team. I do not feel that any useful purpose will be served by my making any further comment.'

ALL THAT REMAINS WHEN THE DUST SETTLES is sediment of hurt and bitterness.

'You don't know how close we came to pulling it off,' Quinn says, the strain of the week writ large on his face. 'It's been a terrible saga, one that's changed all of our lives. Less than three weeks ago, I was waving at fans. I was Mister Nice Guy. Not anymore. But you know, I've a picture of my family beside my 'phone up there in my room. And every phone call I made to Michael Kennedy this week, every time I'd go to Mick's room to pester him about Roy, at the risk probably of causing big problems within the squad, I looked at that picture and I said, "I know they've said to me to do the right thing." And I did the right thing as far as I'm concerned.'

Quinn is angry. In his desperation to find some sign that he had softened his position, he missed a line Keane had used in his RTÉ interview, which Quinn now says was calculated to hurt him in particular. Certain players in the squad, Keane said, were worried about their reputations, having sensed a shift in the Irish public's opinion over who was to blame for what happened. His own motives, Quinn says, were unselfish.

'I thought we could still be one big happy ship again. I was doing it for Roy Keane. I was doing it for the people of Ireland. And for Mick McCarthy as well – that big, rough, gruff, tough man who had an eleventh-hour change of heart.

'I'll never understand why he [Keane] just didn't make a lukewarm attempt and ring Mick, because I think at that stage of the game it's all it would have taken. Michael Kennedy said at one stage in our negotiations that if Roy didn't apologise and just rang Mick to say he was coming, would that be enough? I said no, because I didn't want to upset Mick. But I said, "Just tell him to make the call and between them I'd say Mick would almost be as relieved as anybody that he did. And then let them work it out." And that's how close we were getting. Roy just wouldn't stand down. And anyone who knows him would say, that's Roy Keane.

'As for protecting my reputation, I would think I've left it in tatters, well maybe not in tatters, but very much open to question by the media by what I've done this week. I went out strongly to bat for Roy. I tried to get him back and it was a close thing. But I sit easy knowing that if I was a coward, which he called me, I'd have come away after the press conference I gave on Tuesday and given up. I didn't give up. I carried on trying to get Roy back throughout the night, right up until five minutes before the call finally came through that Roy wouldn't be coming after all.

'I personally hope that he wears the green shirt for Ireland again. And I'll tell you something, no matter what part of the world I'm living in, I'll fly and go to that game and watch our best player, if not our greatest-ever player, I'll bring my kids to watch him play for his country again.'

THREE DAYS BEFORE IRELAND PLAY CAMEROON, Quinn is asked about the mood in the camp. He says that on the bus to training the day before, one player turned to him and said: 'I watched Italia '90 as a kid and I dreamt about going to the World Cup. It wasn't supposed to be like this.' It could have been anyone. And everyone.

NO REGRETS. Somebody wrote it on the chalkboard in the dressing room and now, as the players stand in a defiant huddle in the middle of the pitch, arms around one another in brotherhood, Steve Staunton uses the words as his final benediction. 'No regrets,' he says. This is his *Braveheart* moment. He has never much loved the sound of his own voice, but after all that's happened there are things that need saying. Think about the effort it took us to get this far, he says. Remember Amsterdam and Lisbon. Remember Tehran. Remember Portugal and Holland in Dublin. Then there are things that don't need saying. Back home the people are angry that Keane is watching this on television. From friends and family, the players know about the demonstration outside the FAI's offices. In the popular mind, they know, they are a one-man team who will be exposed for what they are against Cameroon in Niigata this afternoon.

'Don't be shy,' Staunton says. 'Express yourselves. Don't anybody hide out there. Remember, no regrets.'

McCarthy sits on the bench, his legs crossed, his pen playing nervously on his lips while he waits for the kick-off. A backing-track of bongos and bodhráns fills his ears. Patrick Mboma and Samuel Eto'o tip off and edge the ball back to Rigobert Song, who hits it high and forward. Ian Harte puts his head on it. In the tense, uncertainty-filled opening minutes, everyone will want to get their first touch out of the way, but no one will know what to do with it. McAteer heads it to Kilbane, who, in a nervous moment, controls it with his hand and gives away a free-kick.

The match is slow to define itself in its first tentative minutes. The players fence cautiously, killing time with backwards and sideways passes. If Roy Keane were here, he'd hit someone with a big haymaker of a challenge, like he did Marc Overmars in Dublin, to remind everyone what a big day it is. If Roy Keane were here …

Marc Vivien Foe spins away from Mark Kinsella and the ball works loose. Foe and Matt Holland have the same ground to make up to reach it. They arrive at the same time, Holland with more conviction. Crunch. He puts the ball out of play and Foe into orbit, then jumps to his feet and makes the shape of a ball with his hands. The referee agrees with him. Foe stays on the ground, but gets only a throw-in for his theatrics. Lauren grabs Holland by the shoulder and pushes him away. Holland looks around him and claps. He's thinking, 'Come on, lads. Wake up.'

Cameroon are true to type: fit, physical and skilful. For forty-five minutes they are the better team, dictating the pace with their clever inventiveness and neatly parsed passing movements. Lauren, Geremi, Foe and Pierre Wome share the ball between them, using the entire width of the pitch, while up front Mboma and Eto'o show off their repertoire of feints and flicks. Holland charges full-bore into another tackle, this time on Wome, but most of his team-mates are paying Cameroon silent respect. Damien Duff and Robbie Keane poke around enthusiastically at the other end of the pitch, but their impress is light. Against Bill Tchato, Rigobert Song and Raymond Kalla, they are just a couple of Davids facing three sturdy Goliaths. Unbiblical odds. They are being roughed up.

Kalla ambles out of defence with the ball as far as the halfway line, then inches a short pass forward to Eto'o, who exchanges a quick one-two with Mboma. Suddenly he's in oceans of space and speeding away, Breen marooned in his wash. Only Shay Given is left to be beaten. Given charges off his line and prepares to launch himself at the ball. The excitement gets to Eto'o, whose second touch is too firm and he ends up having to stretch to shoot with the outside of his right boot. Given dives on top of it as he might a burning man. He smothers the shot. Gary Kelly cleans up.

At the other end, one of the Davids enjoys a rare success. McAteer plays a short corner to Harte, who hangs a cross in the air. Tchato waits for Song to clear it. Song looks at Tchato. Keane, six inches smaller than either of then, insinuates himself in between them and puts his forehead on the ball. It bounces a foot wide of the post. Incensed, Boukar Alioum, the Cameroon goalkeeper, kicks the post and performs a petulant little dance on the spot. Tchato tells him he's sorry.

Kinsella has begun to throw himself into challenges. By the middle of the first-half a chant of, 'Are you watching, Roy Keane?' has spread like a bush-fire around the stadium. Whoever has started it, though, isn't following the narrative of the match. The Irish players are living on their nerves. Kalla tests the flight of the ball from thirty yards, which Given saves. Then Foe takes a turn but gets the trajectory wrong and his shot sails over the bar. In between, Harte gives the ball away carelessly to Mboma who, from a confounding angle out on the right, tries to chip Given.

Seven minutes before half-time, the goal that Cameroon have been threatening to score arrives. Foe plays a tidy pass to Geremi, who looks up to see Eto'o making a diagonal run from the D of the Irish penalty box to the right flank. Staunton dutifully follows, sticking closely behind. Eto'o shields the ball and takes it, in a broad arc, as far as the byline. Staunton tries to run him out of play, but Eto'o is too clever for him. With his third touch he pulls the ball back from the line and through Staunton's legs. Staunton falls over, then rolls onto his stomach to see Eto'o poke the ball back to Mboma with his toe. Given is helpless, his goal gaping wide. Mboma lets the ball come across him, stops it with his instep and slides it into the goal, despite Holland and Kelly's despairing efforts to keep it out. Given punches the air and practices his withering look for the benefit of no one in particular. Then he goes off to fish the ball out of the net. Mboma takes off his shirt and lays it on the ground and the Cameroon players perform a natty little raindance around it.

Three minutes later, Ireland are back on the ropes and awaiting the final punch that will send them off to sleep. Kilbane is carrying the ball out of defence when he is mugged by Geremi. His cross is met first time by Mboma, whose volley is a foot too high and wide. Then, against the run of play, Ireland create a chance. Duff wins a free-kick to the right of the Cameroon penalty box. Kalla and Salomon Olembe are detailed to make a wall in front of him. Harte raises his arm to signal some recondite plan of action, then whips the ball into the box with his left foot. The kick is poor. The ball is heading harmlessly for the near post, until Song attacks it, then watches in horror as it hits his left foot and spins, in slow time, towards his own goal. It partly crosses the line. But Alioum drops to his left and stops it before it alights on the other side. Song is shaken up. The climb that Ireland face in the second-half suddenly seems a bit less severe.

FROM A BAR IN MALTA, GARY BREEN watched Ireland's first World Cup adventure come to an end. Worn out after his GCSEs, he and a gang of friends went on a sun holiday and spent most of the daylight hours sitting in pubs, watching the football. Breen, in his chowder-thick Kentish Town accent, cheering for Ireland, the country of his All Ireland-winning great-grandfather, of childhood holidays in Kerry and of the father who took him to Croke Park to see Páidí Ó Sé, the Spillanes and Bomber Liston. The night that Ireland played Italy there was no confusion about where he was from. That glorious, ambrosial June of twelve summers ago, Breen wore his love of Ireland on his sleeve.

'I remember the shot from Donadoni – had a bit of swerve on it – Packie not being able to hold it and Schillaci scoring. We were one game away from the semi-finals and it's only now, looking back on it, that you realise that Ireland could have even gone and won it.'

The moral of that World Cup campaign has been borne out in this one: spirit and organisation can get you places. In the six years since his début for Ireland, Breen's watched enough big summer tournaments on television to know what it means to be here.

'Not qualifying is terrible, but you don't appreciate how terrible until the tournament actually starts and you're not there. I remember watching the last World Cup, seeing Belgium playing and thinking that should have been us there. I watched Euro 2000 on the telly thinking Yugoslavia weren't any better than us and nor were Turkey.

'Personally, the lowest I've ever felt playing for Ireland was in the changing room after the play-off match in Brussels. We all felt we should've qualified. A lot of the players there I'd watched playing for Ireland in the World Cup when I was a teenager, and not getting to France '98 was the end of many of their careers. It was a transitional period for the team and the difference now is that if we had to play Belgium again, we'd comfortably beat them.'

He is beanpole thin, seventy-five kilos stretched over a knotty six-foot frame. He has sad cow eyes underscored by little half-moons, a smile full of teeth and a surgeon's mask of black stubble, beneath a tight military crewcut. He is, as Mick McCarthy acknowledges, not everyone's cup of tea. Roy Keane is counted among his critics. When Ireland were labouring to beat Cyprus in Nicosia, the camera caught Keane roaring at him as they walked off the pitch at half-time. Breen had the fear of the bullied child on his face. Can he put words to the picture?

'Can't remember that one,' he says, as though it happens too often for him to take it personally. 'I think it might have been a bad pass I gave him.' Did he make the mistake again that night? 'He makes you concentrate, put it that way. You know you can't get away with mistakes when he's playing in front of you.'

Before this began, Breen was the player that Irish fans grumbled about most, a player who punctuated even his best performances with a couple of moments when his mind would absent itself and an opponent would be presented with a chance. Most importantly though, he *is* the manager's cup of tea. McCarthy stood by him, even in the dark days when he was fighting with Gordon Strachan, his former boss at Coventry.

'It was difficult coming away to play for Ireland at that stage,' he says. 'If you're not getting your game with your club, you start thinking, "Should I really be here at all? Am I taking somebody else's place?"'

McCarthy wasn't picking him for sentiment's sake, but his belief in him meant a lot. 'I don't really talk to Mick on the 'phone, or anything like that,' he says. 'We don't have that kind of relationship. But he's an honest man and I like that. He tells you when you're doing well and when you're not doing well. Even when that stuff was going on with my old boss, I never lost my belief in myself and he never lost belief in me either.'

He suffered his growing pains along with McCarthy's team and celebrated his coming-of-age with them as well. The night he felt they were finally all grown-up was the night of the 2-2 draw in Amsterdam. For an hour they gave the game's so-called sophisticates a lesson in how to pass the ball, and he remembers wishing he was at the other end of the pitch, where all the fun was happening. It was one of those rare nights when the former star striker for Westwood Boys of Camden Town regretted reinventing himself as a centre-half.

In his first incarnation, Breen was 'Quinnesque', a great, loping totem-pole of a striker in whose direction his team-mates would launch long balls. But at thirteen his life was turned upside down when a tumour was discovered in his lower spine. He spent six months confined to bed. His most vivid memory of his teenage years is waking up long before the light of dawn had fingered the curtains and hearing his parents getting up to work the extra hours that paid for his visits to Harley Street. He was told that he might never walk again. The tumour was removed. After an excruciating two-week wait, he was told it was benign. By the time he returned to Westwood Boys, the team was already well-off for strikers, so he gravitated towards the area of greatest need. The team was shipping a lot of goals at the back.

Not long after his GCSEs and his summer in Malta, Charlton Athletic offered him an apprenticeship, which he turned down in favour of doing his A-Levels. His first wage slip from football was from Fourth Division Maidstone, who didn't mind if his schoolwork kept him away from training midweek once he showed his face on Saturday. From there he set about making his ascent of the divisions, from Maidstone to Gillingham, to Peterborough, to Birmingham, to Coventry, and never a backward step taken.

He was always ahead of his time: captain of Peterborough at twenty years of age, and playing for the Ireland under-21 team at the age of eighteen. He had so much latent talent back then that England tried to claim him, mistaken in their belief that just because he was born there he considered himself English. Damien Richardson, his manager at Gillingham, told him about the approach in his office one morning.

'You've been called up to the England under-18 squad,' he said.

'I don't want to play for England,' Breen told him.

'Well that's a relief,' Richardson said, 'because I already answered for you. Didn't know if there was any point even telling you.'

A SLOW ACCRUAL OF INCIDENTS suggests the course of the match is changing. McCarthy is forced to reshuffle the team when McAteer admits to him in the dressing room that he was never fit enough to play. There is no time to show his anger. Steve Finnan, who had surprisingly been dropped for Gary Kelly, is told that he's playing the second-half. He takes his place at right-back and Kelly is shunted forward to the right side of midfield. Finnan and Harte begin to scare the Cameroon players with their daring runs forward. Harte curls a cross into the box, which Kilbane glances across the face of the goal and wide. It's a bad miss.

But the match turns on two incidents within sixty fast-flicking seconds, six minutes after the restart. Given throws the ball short to Harte, who starts carrying the ball out of defence. Geremi is closing in on him fast. Harte considers hitting it long to Duff, or Keane. Then he thinks he'll err on caution's side and pass it wide to Staunton. And the longer he procrastinates, the closer Geremi gets and the quicker his options close. He turns around and thinks about laying the ball back to Given. But he is frozen with nerves and he has lost the mastery of his legs. He does nothing. His knees seem to buckle for a second as Geremi filches the ball from his toe and then blasts it in the direction of the goal. Harte sees it fly wide, a relieved man. He thinks, 'Concentrate.'

From the kick-out, Given bypasses him this time, hitting it long to Kilbane who, in one fluid movement, kills the ball on his chest and knocks it five yards ahead. He takes one touch and bends the ball into the penalty box. It's a poor cross, chest-high and nowhere near any of his team-mates. Kalla stoops low to clear it, but fails to get any purchase on his header. The ball stops just outside the box in front of Holland, who hits an untouchable shot that skims across the ground, like a pebble on a still lake, and squeezes just inside the post. A grin flexes across Holland's face and he sets off, his arm aloft in celebration.

The Cameroon players lose their collective nerve in the same way that Harte did moments earlier. Every Irish player wants the ball. They are ravenous for it. Keane and Duff are a blizzard of movement. Tchato, Kalla and Song, the three identikit giant African defenders, look unsure of themselves. With a shuffle of his hips, Duff turns Song and sends a frisson of excitement through the crowd. Kilbane hits a deep cross from the left. Breen is up like a salmon to head the ball across the face of the goal. Kalla swings his foot at it and misses. With Keane bearing down on him, the ball hits Song's midriff and looks certain to go in, but Alioum again pulls the ball back from the line. Duff is like a loose horse, charging around and making a nuisance of himself. Kalla gives in and resorts to fouling him. Duff pits his jaw, bares his teeth. He is thinking, 'They're not the team we thought they were.'

Eto'o, still a dangerously spectral presence, ghosts past Breen again but blazes his shot wide. But the Irish players know the game is there if they want it. Kelly switches to the left side of defence after Harte succumbs to cramp. He comes as far as the halfway line and slides the ball to Keane, who in turn lays it off to Kilbane. He hits it straight away and finds Duff, who runs his foot over it, taunting Kalla for his lack of grace. For a couple of seconds they stand facing one another; Kalla transfixed by the ball at Duff's feet, Duff goading him to make a tackle. Duff's imagination is a full second quicker than Kalla's reflexes. He drops his shoulder, sweeps the ball into a metre of space and crosses it. Tchato's anaemic clearance gets as far as Keane, who takes the ball under control and hits it hard from the edge of the box. He thinks it's destined for the bottom corner and, in his mind, is already rehearsing his celebration. But it changes its mind and cannons off the foot of the post. Alioum is thinking, 'Today, God is on my side.'

The referee spreads his arms wide and blows his whistle. The Irish players share a look of triumphant relief. They could have won, but after what they've been through, the victory is in not losing. They don't want to know how Roy Keane would see it. It's a point won.

MATT HOLLAND WAS ALREADY PUSHING TWENTY-EIGHT when he made his first appearance for Ireland in the dying throes of the Euro 2000 campaign. So where has he been all our lives? The answer is, where *hasn't* he been? No other player on the Irish team has spent as many years soldiering in unglamorous parts to get here. No other player has suffered the knock-backs he has and yet remained as sincere and as wholesome as the choir-boy haircut and child's eyes suggest. Just about everyone with experiences like his got real years ago and packed football in for a proper job.

He spent a short and unhappy period at the Southampton Centre of Excellence when he was ten. Four years later, he had a trial with Arsenal. So did lots of kids. They cast their nets wider than most clubs. They took a good, long look and decided he was too small. They threw him back. In his mind he had just about settled for a life of non-league football and a career in the bank, like his dad, when West Ham offered him an audition. He passed it. Then he kicked his heels for a few years, waiting for them to give him a role in the big production. Before he knew it, he was nearly twenty-one. Mature decisions had to be made. He'd have to lower his sights.

Second Division Bournemouth were offering to take him on loan. Holland tends to see the silver lining and completely miss the cloud. At least he'd be playing football, even if it wasn't at the end of the rainbow. Bournemouth, as it turned out, was anything but. There was no gold. There was no money. No sooner had Holland's move become permanent than the club got itself into financial bother. The players were paid only when there was money in the pot. Weeks went by without any wages. Self-preservation would have told most players to bail out. Holland stayed and, as captain, became the spokesman for the players in their dealings with the press.

But it was serious. He was twenty-five. His wife, Paula, had just had the first of their two sons. The receivers were his white knight. After the football ground, he was Bournemouth's most valuable asset. In the summer of 1997, Ipswich Town offered stg£700,000 for him, with another stg£100,000 on top depending on how many first-team appearances he made. For Holland, it meant First Division football. For Ipswich, it was a steal. His drive and honest work ethic in midfield spearheaded the club's return to the top division and their qualification for the UEFA Cup in their first season back.

Moving again didn't bother him. Wanderlust

comes with the Holland genes. His grandmother on his dad's side came from County Monaghan and worked as a caterer all over England. And his father's career as a bank manager meant they were accustomed to towing their life's possessions up and down the motorways of England as he transferred from one branch to another.

Holland stayed put at Ipswich for five years, racking up two hundred consecutive league appearances, an achievement that makes him something of a freak. Never injured. Never suspended. Never dropped. Captain's armbands seemed to be handed over to him as a matter of course. But he waited so long for an international call-up that he had begun to believe it would never come. When he joined the Irish squad in 1999, what struck him first was the complete devotion that McCarthy commanded from his players. 'Especially the younger ones,' he says, 'the ones he gave a start to, or maybe showed loyalty to over the years, you could see that they would have done anything for him.'

His début came on a day that McCarthy would like to have surgically removed from his past if he could. Ireland were back in Skopje, needing to beat Macedonia to qualify for Euro 2000. They were quite competently holding on to a one-nil lead when McCarthy decided to make a change. There would have been far wiser moments to hand a player his international début than with a team defending a lead with five minutes to go. Changes can unsettle teams, leave players confused as to who they're supposed to be marking. It was another lesson McCarthy learned the hard way.

Four minutes into injury time, Macedonia scored from a corner and Holland and the rest of his new team-mates watched the tournament at home on television.

All players being fit and present, Holland would not have started a match for Ireland before these finals. Now he's as good as indispensable. For two-and-half years he was a stunt-double for Roy Keane and Mark Kinsella, a sort of Roy Keane Lite and not in any disparaging way.

'When Roy is missing, we don't miss him that much because of Matt,' was one of McCarthy's little white lies. But to see how much Holland has developed these past two years – the indefatigable running, his authority on the ball – is to see how much he's learned at Keane's feet.

'You can't but learn from watching what he does,' he says. 'It's bound to rub off on you.'

McCarthy threw Holland on at half-time in the qualifier in Lisbon. Ireland might have been more than a goal down, but a point was there to be taken.

He asked him to sit just in front of the back four to allow Keane and Kinsella to get forward more. What that meant was marking Luis Figo and making sure Portugal didn't score again. It was a masterful tactical switch by McCarthy. Not only did Holland help stop Portugal getting another, he struck a shock equaliser from outside the box that earned the team an invaluable point.

'What were you doing down that end of the field?' McCarthy said, a smile playing on his lips, when Holland returned to the dressing room. 'I thought I told you to stay back.'

Unsure of his place in the team three months before the World Cup began, he's being talked about now as the next Irish captain. In everything he does he demonstrates his natural instinct to lead. At a press conference at the team's training base in the country town of Izumo, a local journalist asked, in all earnestness, what the team thought of the local water supply. From most players the question would have elicited a quizzical look and a flippant shrug of the shoulders. While the rest of the room sniggered, Holland held forth for five minutes about the importance of water in any team's preparation, and how the local issue had been 'absolutely tremendous, to be fair.'

Keane may be gone now, but the team won't want for leaders.

A TELEVISION CREW ARRIVE AT THE IRISH TEAM'S HOTEL one afternoon to interview McCarthy for German television. They ask if they can conduct it in the hotel bar, with the Irish manager perched on a high stool with a pint of Guinness in front of him. He looks at them speculatively. More of your German senses of humour, surely. But they're serious.

'No, I will not,' he fumes. 'What the hell do you think we are? A bunch of Paddies going off on our holidays? This is serious, you know.'

Roy Keane would have been proud of him.

IT'S STEVE STAUNTON'S NIGHT and he's determined that nobody else is going to be the centre of attention. No Irish player has ever won a hundred caps before and Staunton starts like he intends making every minute memorable. He needs to. Germany put eight goals past Saudi Arabia in their last match. In the opening minutes Staunton introduces himself to the man who scored three of them, the spiky-haired Miroslav Klose. They both jump for a high ball, their backs to one another. Klose puts all of his body into the challenge. Staunton wins it, then gives him a look of reproach. And if Carsten Jancker, the other German striker, doesn't know who he is, he soon does. Whack. Staunton prostrates him on the ground. Now they both have his card. The referee tells him to calm down.

The atmosphere in the intimate little stadium in Ibaraki spits and crackles. The high stakes are evident in the frantic start that both sides make. Bernd Schneider, the German midfielder, squanders possession and Duff embarks on a mazy run that tests the wits of Christoph Metzelder and Thomas Linke, two of the three German central defenders who will see quite a lot of his back tonight. The third, Carsten Ramelow, a tall sentinel, heads a Kilbane cross clear. At the other end, Breen does something similar. For ten minutes the game is played in the air. Torsten Frings sweeps a cross into the penalty box, which Jancker heads straight into Given's arms. He'll get little more out of Breen and Staunton tonight.

Kelly plays the ball forward to Duff, who goes on another run. Dietmar Hamann chases after him but can't keep up. Their arms become entangled. Duff still manages to get a cross in. Keane homes in on it, but Oliver Kahn gets there first. Square head, blond hair, Aryan features – the German goalkeeper is the impenetrable rock that he looks. Schneider has the ball now on the edge of the Irish box. He flicks it with the outside of his right boot to Klose, who heads for the six-yard box. Staunton sticks to him and decides he's not going to repeat the mistake he made against Cameroon. He slides in. It's reckless. He knows the risk. If he makes contact with Klose, then it only takes a persuasive dive to earn the Germans a penalty. Staunton misses the ball and Klose affects a trip over his leg. The referee scores him zero for artistic merit. Staunton is furious. He shouts at the referee, then turns back to Klose, stands threateningly close to him and tells him he's a cheat.

The Germans are quickest to find their stroke and Hamann is exerting a greater influence over the game the longer it goes on. The Irish players are having difficulty holding onto the ball. It's no surprise when, in the nineteenth minute, they fall behind. Finnan takes a throw-in to Holland, whose pass to Duff is cut out by Metzelder. The ball is worked to Schneider, who's in enough acreage of space to consider his next move. He goes right, fakes a movement with his arm, but doesn't play the ball. He changes direction, sees Ballack to his left and rolls the ball to him. Ballack is a master strategist. There are few players who read the game better than he does. With his first touch, he takes the ball under his spell and knocks it just ahead of himself. His chin goes up as he considers what's happening up ahead. He doesn't look down again – and doesn't need to – until the moment he makes contact with the ball and sends a forty-yard chip into the Irish penalty box. There is pure hubristic arrogance in the pass. Staunton is the only Irish player alive to what is happening. He has followed Hamann's decoy run to the left, leaving his own station unmanned. Harte should cover him, but he's having one of his narcoleptic moments. Staunton sees what's coming before the ball leaves Ballack's boot. He screams at Harte, points to where he should be standing. Too late, though. Klose times his run perfectly. The ball comes down. Only the rarest touch from his head is needed to put it past Given. The move is beautifully choreographed. Klose performs a somersault. McCarthy is mad. He will not criticise any of his players in public, but he knows that lack of concentration has just cost his team a goal. Against Germany, it's difficult to make up any kind of forfeit.

Kahn's battle with Ireland's two front men is becoming one of the game's best subplots. Holland charges down a shot by Schneider and Keane lobs the ball forward to Duff. Linke, Ramelow and Metzelder are caught standing statuesque, looking for a flag. Duff's run is ill-timed, but the linesman decides he is somehow onside and now Duff and Kahn are involved in a race for the ball, over by the left touch-line. Duff is sure he can get to it first. Once he leaves his penalty box, Kahn knows he has to. When he gets there, he opens his body and throws himself at the ball. It rebounds back off Duff for a German throw-in. Duff thinks, 'The guy is good.'

Twenty-five minutes into the first-half, the rain

comes. The ball is oily, so Kahn chooses to punch away a corner. Staunton wins it back. He plays it to Kinsella, who rolls it out left to Harte. Breen tries to get a flick onto his cross but misses, and Linke clears. Holland is in his usual place, on the edge of the penalty box, waiting for a stray ball. He hits it, hard and true, but it zips just wide of Kahn's right-hand post. Staunton is playing like a man who wants to remember every minute of this night. He charges down a shot by Jancker and the ball spins into the air. He goes up after it – a dog catching a Frisbee. He beats Ramelow to the header and before he lands he's already complaining to the referee about having the German's elbow in his chest.

Ireland, though, are going through a period of *ennui*. Their passes keep finding the wrong feet and the Germans are being given time to stroke the ball around. Christian Ziege, fearsome-looking with his mohican and pock-marked face, takes a throw-in deep in the Irish half. The marking is poor. Hamann plays the ball into the box to Ballack, who immediately lays it back to him. Hamann sends in a searing low shot that Given has to hit the floor to save. If Roy Keane were here …

At half-time Breen, like Staunton, won't need to be told to start winning his personal battles. He is wired. He is *in the zone*, in the parlance of the game.

In the huddle before the match he kept interrupting Staunton's pep talk. He couldn't stop himself. We have a responsibility to everyone back home, he said. When you come off the pitch, he said, you can never have that time again, so seize the day. They had to shush him up.

The ball is slipped through to Jancker, the giant, dome-headed striker, and Breen holds him off brilliantly. A few minutes later, Jancker gives voice to his frustration. He tears at Breen's shirt in a chase for the ball and is penalised. He screams at the referee. His face is pure rage.

'You *did* pull my shirt,' Breen says.

'Fuck off,' Jancker shouts at him, and Breen knows Jancker won't score today.

Just before half-time, the Irish players snap out of their reverie. Finnan chips the ball into the box, Linke carelessly heads the ball backwards and Keane tries an overhead kick. It's a difficult skill to execute. Keane gets it wrong, but Staunton claps, offers him encouragement.

ROBBIE KEANE IS SMALL, but he takes up a lot of room in the world. He has always had difficulty sitting still. As a kid he was everywhere. He hated school, couldn't concentrate. He had an attention deficit before anyone thought to call it a disorder. It was football's fault. And Mick McCarthy, in his own way, was an accessory. The boy was never right after Italia '90. The causes of the First World War, the reproductive system of the spirogyra and the principal industries of the Benelux countries could go hang after that. He'd arrive home from school and throw his bag in a corner, where it would remain until first light, then he was off out, booting the ball around the roads. The Grove would play The Gardens, front gates serving as goalposts. There is hardly a neighbour who isn't proud to say that they had their front window put in by Robbie Keane.

These days he rattles around in a five-bedroomed, interior-designed house just outside Leeds, drives a BMW X5 jeep or, when the mood takes him, his Jaguar XK8. Yet his first four words to describe himself would be 'ordinary guy from Tallaght'. He is twenty-one but he has an older man's face, a generous forehead and chin, a fringe that affects a calf's lick, a diamond stud in his left ear and eyes that skitter around like they're trying to pick a face out of a crowd. 'Whacker' they call him, a straight, honest-to-God Dublin nickname.

His dad, Robbie, is a singer. Pubs, clubs, music venues, he's been around the circuit more times than a lurcher. It was from him that Robbie inherited his sense of showmanship. The cartwheel and tumble that he adds like a signature to every goal he scores is flamboyant enough to make Prince Naseem look shy. It comes as no surprise to hear that the celebration routine came long before he ever made it big. He started doing it at Crumlin United. He had left Fettercairn, the local club, to try to get himself noticed. There was little chance of him ever being missed. He was cocky, never ran shy of speaking up for himself, and in front of goal he was unstoppable.

He went from joining Crumlin to making his début for Ireland in the time it takes for a World Cup to come around. He was seventeen when McCarthy gave him his first cap, in a friendly against the Czech Republic in 1998.

'A lot of people would be afraid to take that gamble,' he says. He might owe McCarthy for the belief he showed in him later on, but giving him his first cap wasn't much of a leap of faith. He was having an outstanding first season at Wolves, scoring not only lots of goals but brilliant ones too. He was hot. Ireland had always struggled to produce strikers. There was only Don Givens, Frank Stapleton and Niall Quinn to show for the past twenty-five years. Eoin Hand and Jack Charlton went searching the lowlands of the English football league, looking for second- and third-generation Irishmen to get goals. Tony Cascarino and John Aldridge were on their way out and, though he would remain puzzlingly loyal to him, McCarthy knew that David Connolly was not the answer.

Keane had been level-headed enough at fifteen to choose Wolves ahead of Liverpool, the team he followed as a boy. He would make a patient ascent up the ladder. When he'd done everything he wanted to at Wolves, he moved to Coventry City. It was sensible. Steady as she goes. Then the boss, Gordon Strachan, came to him one morning after training and told him that Inter Milan had made the club an offer for him that might be too good to refuse. It's difficult to tell a lad of nineteen that it's too much too young. Playing in Serie A was the chance of a lifetime. It was never going to be thrown back. He went to Italy, learned enough of the language to get by and joined the queue of world stars looking to get into the team. It all ended as suddenly as it had begun. Marcelo Lippi, the man who bought him, got the sack. Marco Tardelli arrived and cleared out what had belonged to the old man. It's the way of things in Italy.

Keane returned to England, to Leeds United. For the first time in his short life he'd been asked to take a backward step. It didn't affect him at first. He just went on scoring goals. Then they stopped going in. He seemed to have lost his touch. It was very evident when he played for Ireland. He headed them into the lead in Amsterdam, then didn't score again for more than a year. He played against Cyprus, Andorra, Estonia – the kind of teams that helped international strikers pad out their goal-scoring records – but he couldn't put the ball in the net.

At Leeds he slipped out of the first team. 'This is the first English club he's been at where he isn't an automatic pick anymore,' the manager, David O'Leary said. Mark Viduka and Alan Smith started ahead of him and, for the first time in his life, Keane was being asked to sit still. It made him unhappy. He was playing fifteen minutes here, ten minutes there. McCarthy never criticised him.

'Robbie doesn't need to prove his ability to me,' he said. 'There's absolutely nothing he needs to show me.'

Then, in April 2001, he turned his ankle against Arsenal and was out for a month. He came back heavier, his lack of fitness evident in his jowls. McCarthy played him against Portugal in Dublin at the end of May – a mistake, as Keane was clearly unready.

'Robbie is a world-class striker,' McCarthy said. 'It will come for him again. I know that.'

O'Leary said much the same thing, then went out and bought Robbie Fowler. Keane spent large parts of his second season at Leeds watching games pass him by. He would knock on O'Leary's door and put his case. No better man for it. With McCarthy he never had to, though in private, Keane says, McCarthy offers players more than just an arm around the shoulder. 'Whether you play well or not, he always gives you a kick up the rear end.'

The goal that McCarthy said would come, did. Keane volleyed the decisive second goal against Iran in Dublin. Fourteen months after scoring the first goal of the qualifiers, he scored the last. Long overdue, but worth waiting for. And with the promise of more to come.

A GOAL UP AT HALF-TIME, Germany declare their innings and Ireland go chasing the game. Harte hits a long ball forward. Keane scampers after it. Metzelder is clever. He runs right across Keane's flight path, allowing the ball to run harmlessly out of play. Keane takes a handful of his shirt and Metzelder swings an elbow at him. They stand toe to toe, glowering at one another, Keane a whole head shorter. He is thinking, 'I don't care how big you are.' Kahn parts them, rescuing Metzelder.

Holland follows Ballack so determinedly that the German may need a court injunction to get rid of him afterwards. Finnan advances deep into the German half and hits a cross, which is cleared as far as Kinsella. He tells Finnan to try again and rolls the ball back to him. This time he gets the right direction on it. Kilbane heads it on in the penalty box. Duff has already started his run. Linke tugs on his arm, but Duff throws him off. He's ten yards out and about to score. Kahn leaps in front of him, making a star shape with his body. The bigger he makes himself, the greater the chances of the ball hitting some part of his anatomy. Duff catches the ball on the volley, but the ball catches Kahn on the backside and bounces away from the goal.

With grim stubbornness, the Germans defend their lead. Duff is their biggest concern. On the start sheet it said he was a centre-forward, but his instinct is to wander and it's difficult to keep track of him. When he shows up on the right wing, the Germans don't ask whose responsibility he is; Ramelow, Ziege and Metzelder all crowd in on him together. But as the time passes, so Ireland's frustration grows. Defeat means almost certain elimination. The crowd knows it. The irritation mounts in Keane. He kicks Hamann; he will have to be careful.

The Germans are capable of scoring a second on one of their occasional sorties into the Irish half. Ballack misses with a shot from thirty yards after an hour, then slips a pass to Jancker around the back of Staunton, who is left standing stock-still. Jancker is in on goal, on the right side of the penalty box. Finnan thinks about cutting across to put pressure on him, but there isn't time enough to get there. Besides, Given is already on his way. Finnan checks back and covers the goal line. Given throws himself in front of Jancker, who manages to lift the ball over him, but Finnan is there to watch it bounce past the post.

With twenty minutes to go, McCarthy takes a gamble. He abandons his efforts to pick the lock and opts for Plan B of booting the door off its hinges. Niall Quinn is sent on. Harte is sacrificed, Kilbane pushed back to left-back and Duff moved to the left wing. Steven Reid takes Kelly's place on the right side of midfield. It's the final throw. With a big man playing next to Keane, Ireland have opened up a new front. Kilbane reaches him with a beautifully struck long ball into the box, which Quinn flicks on with a delicate touch for Keane. Kahn throws himself at his feet to make the save again. Then Breen nods the ball weakly wide. When Kahn saves another shot from Keane with his chest with two minutes to go, the Irish players believe they're on their way out of the World Cup.

Kinsella is thinking, 'We've tried everything.' Finnan is thinking, 'Can't be long left now.' Duff is thinking, 'It's gone.' The electronic board has been held up to show there are three minutes of injury time to play. At least one of those has already gone.

Then Ballack fails to control a clearance and the ball runs out of play. In his urgency to take the throw-in, Breen can't stop himself running and his momentum brings him crashing into the German bench. Extricating himself from it takes a few seconds. Finnan hits the ball long and high. Quinn beats Metzelder to it with his head and it drops into the penalty box. Keane slips in between Linke and Ramelow. The ball bounces up and hits his thigh and falls, fortuitously, at his feet. Kahn makes himself big. Keane is eight yards out. There's work to be done still. The ball is almost under him and it has to be dug out. He is almost bent double when he hits it. Kahn touches it onto the post, but can't keep it out. The rest of the players are unsighted. Breen thinks it's gone wide. Holland is convinced it went the other side of the post. McCarthy stands with his mouth wide open, unable to believe it's gone in. But Kahn is punching the air in anger and Keane is off, performing his signature celebration. Then he disappears under a press of team-mates who can barely believe it's happened.

WHEN THE FINAL WHISTLE BLOWS, Duff is too engrossed in his own thoughts to go looking for a German to swap shirts with. His mother and father and Jamie, the kid brother who adores him, are somewhere in the sea of green behind the goal, just three of the

10,000 Irish supporters who'd thrilled to his performance.

Back in the dressing room, Johnny Fallon, the team's Mister Fixit, asks him whose shirt he got. Duff says nobody's; he isn't bothered. It stings Fallon a bit. What happened out there tonight was precious. The lad is too young to realise how rarely these nights come along. It's only right that he should have a souvenir of it. So Fallon takes Duff's green shirt and makes off in the direction of the German dressing room. Three minutes later he's back with a crisp white one. He hands it to Duff, who balls it up and stuffs it into his bag, without the slightest curiosity to see whose shirt he got.

For a young man with no regard for reputations, who plays football so unselfconsciously that he almost seems unaware of the stage he's tramping, that's about right. When he's asked about the World Cup, he obliges with the usual reflexive answers about it being the biggest sporting event in the world, the pinnacle of every player's career; then he goes out with a fearlessness that suggests he doesn't really know where he is. His body might be at the World Cup, but his spirit is back at Lourdes Celtic.

The world is raving about him, yet Duff wears a permanent look on his face that suggests he believes the world to be quite mad. He is short, with an untidy thatch of blond hair that won't be tamed by any brush, thick straw eyebrows, narrow shoulders that are always kept slouched and a walk that makes him look like he's carrying an invisible bag filled with rocks hitched to his back. His capacity for sleep has attained legendary status within the squad. Niall Quinn says he would happily sleep for the twenty-two hours of the day when he's not training. 'He can afford to talk,' says Duff.

Defenders are no longer fooled by his somnolent appearance. He is almost impossibly skilful. With a quick shuffle of his feet he can leave the best full-backs in the game kicking at thin air.

He has only faint memories of Mick McCarthy as a player. He had just turned eleven when Italia '90 burst into the family living room in Ballyboden, south Dublin. 'I remember the t-shirts,' he says. 'And the Jackie Charlton songs. And the whole country going wild.'

It made an impression on him, though not such a big one. He joined Leicester Celtic in Dublin that summer, like just about every other kid in the neighbourhood. But when he moved to secondary school, he was persuaded to abandon football for rugby and De La Salle Churchtown's quest for the Leinster Junior Cup. He was a full-back, a good one by some accounts. Then the hormones arrived, unevenly dispensed about the class. Some of his friends sprouted facial hair overnight. Others sprouted a few inches. He stayed the same.

'Everyone was suddenly so much bigger than me,' he says, 'which is when I got back into football.'

He moved to Lourdes Celtic, but every club in Dublin was soon aware of this tiny, fair-headed boy with the sprinter's speed and the tricky feet. Bray Wanderers' manager Pat Devlin saw him play in Sallynoggin one Saturday morning, against St Joseph's Boys. He skipped effortlessly around two players and lobbed the keeper. Devlin was smitten. And Duff was back in love with football and driving his teachers to distraction. What did he want to be when he grew up, they'd ask. Footballer, he'd say. Yes, of course, but what did he *really* want to be. And he'd give them that look: mad.

He took his party piece to St Kevin's Boys in Whitehall. It was a hard slog getting across the city for training and matches, but they were one of the best clubs in the country. It was the place to get noticed. The talent scouts tend to gravitate towards the better-known nurseries and leave the smaller clubs alone. Duff ended up at Blackburn, steered into the arms of the Premiership champions by Devlin, who was a good friend of Kenny Dalglish.

He joined Blackburn on a Youth Training Scheme

and shacked up with his new pals at the club's youth academy. It was all happening like it had in his dreams. At first. Then the homesickness arrived, not immediately, it was something that seeped into his bones like arthritis.

'I was grand at first,' he says. 'There were a lot of Irish lads there at the time and it didn't really hit me that I'd even moved away from home in that first year. Then it started to sink in. It was really bad. I went to see the youth team manager, told him I wanted to go home. He wouldn't let me. He thought it would help me if my family came over. So me Ma and Da came over and stayed with me for about a week and eventually I was grand.'

He was grand enough to make his first-team début just a few weeks after his eighteenth birthday. Dalglish had gone by then, as had Alan Shearer, and the team was foundering. Tony Parkes took over as caretaker manager and stopped the team from being relegated.

'We were officially safe and I was at home in Dublin on me holliers,' he says, 'and Tony rang and called me back. Told me he wanted me to make me début in a match against Leicester.'

A Man of the Match performance earned him the first of many rave reviews. Roy Hodgson took over from Parkes that summer, watched a recording of the match and pronounced Duff the new George Best.

Hodgson, unfortunately, wasn't the new Matt Busby and his time at the club was short. Duff's new boss, Brian Kidd, could find no room for him in his 4-3-3 system with its lack of width, and Duff was relegated to the role of spectator, whether he was on the pitch or not. Many Blackburn supporters considered their relegation in 1999 a direct consequence.

Playing in the First Division was a shock to the system. The whole topography of his life changed. One minute, Old Trafford, Highbury and Anfield were the peaks he gazed up at; the next, he had Walsall, Crewe and Rotherham blotting his landscape.

'It didn't really hit any of us, until a while later, where we were going to be playing next season. You just wanted to get swallowed up a hole then, or go away for God knows how long.'

His international career stuttered like a needle on a scratched record. Blackburn couldn't get any enthusiasm out of themselves the following season and finished tenth in the First Division. That same season, Duff wasn't even on the pitch when a last-minute goal in Macedonia stopped Ireland going to the European Championships.

'Wasn't the best of years for me,' he says. 'I was on a real downer here at Blackburn. A real downer. And then I lost my place in the Irish team and, to be honest with you, I didn't really enjoy going back to

Dublin and meeting up with the squad in those days.'

A new season brought another new boss and stability at last in his career. 'He [Souness] came to me in the middle of his first season here and told me he was dropping me. I asked him why and he said that, with the ability I had, he needed to get more out of me, which I suppose made me more determined.'

It worked. The club returned to the Premiership, with Duff their Player of the Year, and now they've put a stg£25m price on him to ward off interest in him. The big, expansive pitches in Japan have given him a broad canvas on which to show off his talent. Noel O'Reilly, who was Brian Kerr's assistant when Duff played at the World Youth Championships in Malaysia in 1997, isn't surprised by the confidence with which he has expressed himself.

'It's his stage,' he says. 'Ask any great artist where they'd rather show their paintings off – in a classroom, or in the National Art Gallery. The sort of skill he has is precocious. Nobody in England has what he has, the particular style with which he beats players. He's comfortable on his left foot and his right foot and he gets out of tight situations because he has a funny shape to him. He always looks like he's about to hit the deck, but he never does.

'To appreciate just how good he was against Germany, you have to remember how difficult it is to make your name when you're an attacking player playing international football. This is not meant to sound disrespectful to defenders, but there is not as much pressure on them to do well. When you're a player like Damien Duff, there's a person breathing down your neck either side of you. And still the Germans were scared stiff of him. They'd their work done on him, no doubt about that. They'd six players all working at one stage to try to stop him getting the ball.

'Watching him and Robbie, I likened it to two fellas playing down the street, little Robbie and Damien, up against the big kids, being bullied, being boxed around the place. And then they get their big brother. On comes Niall Quinn. "Come on and pick on me," he says to the German defenders, "and while you're doing that, these two little lads will rob your pockets."'

After the match, the players party until dawn invades the bar in the team hotel. O'Reilly's guitar keeps them going through the night. Robbie Keane needs no cajoling to do his party piece, 'Joxer goes to Stuttgart'. Duff surprises everyone with 'Leroy Brown'. What strikes O'Reilly as they say their good mornings and call it a night is how much growing up Keane and Duff have done in the three years since they played together at the World Youth

Championships in Nigeria.

'They gave me a hug,' he says. 'Little memories of the way it was. And I realised then that they're not kids anymore. They're seasoned men, playing against the best players in the world.'

THEY KNOW WHAT THEY WANT. Two goals against Saudi Arabia – by popular consent the worst team in the tournament. The Saudis still have their pride, though. Or at least some desire to get it back. The coach, Nasser Al Johar, has a date with the Saudi royal family when he returns to Riyadh, to try to put into words what's gone wrong. A win in Yokohama tonight would change the tenor of that meeting.

'Against Ireland we will give a proper picture of Saudi football to the world,' he says. They almost shut out Cameroon, who had to wait until the sixty-sixth minute for their only goal. To make certain of qualifying for the next round, Ireland just need to beat their total.

In the first few minutes it looks like no job at all. Straight to business, Keane cracks a shot from thirty yards after only three minutes, but it's charged down. But his first goal is just three minutes away. Kinsella plays a neat pass back to Staunton just inside the Irish half. He stops the ball, takes a cursory look up and hits a forty-yard pass to Kelly, who's charging down the right. There isn't time to take the ball down. Abdullah Zubromawi is on his way to close him down. So he hits it as soon as it's low enough to get his foot to it and it's ballooned high into the Saudi penalty box. Keane anticipated a cross, but he checks back as far as the penalty spot, his eyes never leaving the ball as it descends. Standing side-on to the goal, he catches it before it gets an opportunity to bounce, and the sheer force of the shot takes it under Mohammed Al Deayea's body and over the line.

Twelve thousand Irish supporters go wild with the thrill of having broken the back of the job so soon. Then they settle back in their seats to enjoy the cooling current blowing across the pitch, and they wait hungrily for the next instalment. But it doesn't come. For a long time it all goes ominously quiet.

Hussein Sulimani charges down the left channel and puts over a cross. Nobody is there to meet it. He's furious that his team-mates don't seem to share his ambition. He tells Hasan Al Yami, the Saudi striker, 'We can score against this team,' and the belief slowly suffuses its way through his team. Abdulaziz Khathran hits a shot from thirty-five yards with the outside of his boot, which Given picks out of the air. Nawaf Al Temyat, the brilliant, beak-nosed playmaker, becomes the nodal point of the growing number of Saudi attacks. He must be stopped. But

Holland and Kinsella have gone missing. Ireland look leaderless. And if Roy Keane were on the pitch right now, he'd ...

Al Temyat doesn't want for confidence. Al Yami feeds the ball to him and he's standing on the edge of the Irish penalty box with his back to goal and Breen's breath on his neck. With his first touch he flicks it over both their heads and slips around the back of Breen to retrieve it. There's a bit too much meat on his touch and it's easy for Given. But the Saudis are convinced they will score. Al Yami has the ball on the edge of the Irish penalty box. With a neat shuffle of his feet, he cuts outside Staunton and inside Breen, but takes too long mulling over his shot and Staunton manages to poke the ball away at the second attempt. Al Temyat lets fly, but his shot breezes wide. Then he exposes Harte's struggle with the basic geography of defending with a pass that leaves Al Yami with a clear run on goal. His shot is somehow drawn straight into Given's hands. Ireland go in at half-time still ahead, but only on the scoreboard.

MARC OVERMARS TORMENTED GARY KELLY beyond all dignity in Dublin. It was one of those off-days when nothing went right for him. You didn't need to be an expert on the psychodynamics of defending to know where it was all leading. In the second-half, with Ireland desperately trying to keep Holland out, Kelly upended Overmars for the second time and the referee had no choice but to send him off. He looked a sad shadow of the full-back who had made the Premiership team of the season in 1993 and the Irish team for the World Cup a year later. Banished to the substitutes' bench at Leeds, and with Stephen Carr and Steve Finnan both emerging as world-class right-backs, Kelly's future might have been in doubt. Not in McCarthy's mind. Had Carr been fit, he still would have taken him to Japan. As the squad struggled to come to terms with the loss of Keane, it was Kelly's enthusiasm in training and the high standing in which he's held by the younger players that convinced McCarthy that he should play ahead of Finnan against Cameroon.

'The gaffer said to me that I did well leading up to the World Cup,' he said, 'and so I deserved my chance again.' It's the kind of loyalty that Kelly will sweat pounds to repay.

IT'S RAINING. BUT NOT GOALS. McCarthy decides to take a risk. He tells Harte he's not needed for the second-half. He is the loose thread in the Irish defence and the Saudis will keep worrying at him until the whole garment comes undone. New impetus is needed up front as well. Quinn gets another cameo appearance.

Duff is shifted over to his usual position on the left side of midfield, and Kilbane is asked to fill in at left-back. Ireland are reinvigorated. Freed from the restrictions of playing up front, Duff is suddenly better able to express himself, with long, stream-of-consciousness runs that confuse the Saudis. From inside his own half, he sets off, slaloms his way around Mohammed Al Jahani and Al Sharani, who takes hold of his arm to try to slow him down. Duff shakes free and dispatches a shot, but can't get any power behind it. A minute later, Kilbane plays an adroit back-heel to Duff, who hurdles Al Jahani's challenge and cuts it back to Keane, who has his back to the goal. He stops the ball, pirouettes forty-five degrees, but shoots across the face of the goal. Keane has the energy of a dervish. Every ball is chased, no cause considered lost.

The Saudis aren't done trying. But the game pivots on one moment of defensive carelessness not long after the one-hour mark. Kilbane breaks forward down the left. Al Temyat goes after him and tugs his wrist. Kilbane reaches back and pulls his shirt. Then he goes down. From what, it's difficult to tell. The referee books Al Temyat. The free-kick alone is an injustice. The Saudis are still cavilling about it when Staunton swings the ball into the box. Quinn spins away from Redha Tukar and moves towards the back post, but Tukar doesn't notice. He and Abdulah Zubromawi stand watching the ball, apparently transfixed by it, as it sails towards the six-yard box. Breen senses their hesitation, inveigles himself between them, stretches out a long leg and the ball is in the back of the net again.

The Irish players are unaware that one hundred miles away in Shizouka, Germany are beating Cameroon and a place in the second round is already theirs. Still, they coast through the time that remains, room opening up everywhere, everyone wanting the ball, giddy with the thought that they will be leaving in the morning on a airplane bound for Seoul. Kinsella sweeps one side of the pitch to the other and Kilbane chests it down. Holland is already pointing to where he wants the ball. Kilbane rolls it to him and Holland threads it through to Duff, who accelerates away from Al Jahani and hits his shot straight at the keeper. It's a deceitful shot, though, full of spin. Al Deayea thinks he has it in his hands. A millisecond later it's in the back of the net. Duff runs to the Irish crowd behind the goal, joins his hands together as if in prayer and bows. His way of saying Sayonara.

IT WAS IN A SMALL, MISERABLE DRESSING ROOM in the Stadionul Steaua in Bucharest that Mick McCarthy assumed the role of a father figure in Ian Harte's eyes. It was the last day of April 1997. Ireland had lost a World Cup qualifier to Romania after doing enough to earn a point. Roy Keane missed a penalty in the second-half, but Harte blamed himself. It was from his careless header that Adrian Ilie had scored the only goal of the match and the folly of using a player so raw as a stopgap centre-half was laid bare. He was nineteen years old and better known as Gary Kelly's nephew than as an emerging full-back for Leeds United. What happened might have broken some players. Emotionally, Harte was out on a ledge that night. It was McCarthy who put an arm around him and talked him down.

'I was very upset,' he says. 'I wasn't a centre-half. I knew that. But there was a vacancy there and you're not going to turn down the opportunity to play for your country. I'll never forget that Mick had faith in me when people were putting me down.'

And still they're putting him down. He has long been identified as the faultline in the Irish defence. He is slow. His spatial awareness is poor. But McCarthy has made a catchphrase out of the line, 'Hartey's all right by me.' Asked on the eve of the match against Saudi Arabia what he thought of the criticism of Harte's previous two performances, McCarthy says, 'Tell them to bollocks.' He says: 'I'm not going to accept criticism of any of them. We have a number of players who don't appeal to the public and to journalists. And you fellas have a very powerful armoury in what you can do for players and how you report on them. Dave Connolly's not enjoyed the best of times. Breeny's not enjoyed the best of times. Hartey, when he got in first, was great. Now he gets a bit of stick because people look at what he can't do rather than what he does bring to the party.'

What he brings, most especially, are goals. He is perhaps the best striker of a dead ball in England. His success rate from free-kicks is better than David Beckham's. His record from penalties is near to unblemished. He has scored eight goals for Ireland, with an international goals-to-games ratio almost as good as Niall Quinn's. He scored four goals in the qualifiers, including the decisive opener against Iran in Dublin from the penalty spot. And while McCarthy will tell him off quietly for the things he does wrong, you can trawl through thousands of interviews with the manager and not come up with anything that could be construed as criticism of him. The result is that Harte would probably stop bullets for him if he could.

There is no better example of an Irish player who has blossomed under the unconditional love of McCarthy and the tough love of Keane. There is wonder in Harte's voice when he speaks about Keane and what he has learned watching him. 'He'd make you want to be a better player,' he says. When Kelly was sent off against Holland, the nephew wondered for how much longer they could hold out. 'Roy just took complete charge,' he says, 'started taking the ball out of defence and bringing it down the field, holding it up to give us all a breather.'

Harte is proof that it's possible to have Mick McCarthy *and* Roy Keane as your heroes. In the lonely hours after McCarthy told Keane that he was out of the World Cup squad, only two players knocked on Keane's door to shake his hand, thank him for what he'd done and wish him well. One was McAteer, a player with whom Keane had never got on. The other was Harte. They weren't close either. They never got to know each other particularly well. As Harte said, 'It's difficult to get inside his head and see what he's really like sometimes.' Harte didn't have to go to see him. Keane wouldn't have thought any less of him had he stayed away like the rest. But he didn't. It took guts. Character.

STEVE STAUNTON'S HEAD BOBBLES UP AND DOWN as he offers his final words of encouragement in the huddle. Then Damien Duff and Robbie Keane are standing over the ball, akimbo, awaiting the referee's signal. But there's thirty seconds to go before it's half-past eight in Seoul, and they're told to wait.

The first exchanges are frantic, breathless. Ian Harte throws himself headlong into a tackle. Kevin Kilbane charges down the left wing, but his long, nervous legs betray him. Then Raul finds himself on the edge of the Irish box with options either side of him. De Pedro is brilliantly placed to his left, if he could just prod the ball through to him. Even the great, gangling Real Madrid striker misses things when he's edgy. Staunton, the mortise lock in the Irish defence, takes the ball from him. There is no anxiety about Keane. His next touch, with the match just two minutes old, is a mischievous back-heel to Kilbane, close to the halfway line. He doesn't wait around for congratulations but charges up the left to accept the return, pulls the ball inside to wrong-foot Puyol, adjusts his feet and curls a shot just outside the far post. A minute later, on the far side of the pitch, Duff steps nimbly around Juanfran, one of four Spanish defenders he will sadistically torture this afternoon.

Heartened by their early successes, they lose concentration and suddenly, for the third time in this World Cup, Ireland find themselves a goal behind and chasing the match. Spain win a throw-in after seven minutes, deep in the Irish half. Puyol saunters over to gather up the ball. His speciality is the long throw into the box. Harte is thinking, 'He's going to throw it long,' and he moves into the middle. Puyol breaks the habit of a lifetime and throws it short to the unmarked Luis Enrique. Puyol gets it back, brings it to the byline and sends a cross sailing right over Harte and onto the head of Fernando Morientes, who has insinuated himself in front of Breen. The simple beauty of a well-worked goal. Shay Given is no appreciator. He's angry. It goes without saying how Roy Keane would have felt about it.

Once again Ireland are looking to get back to the position from which they started, roared on by a crowd of fans that has more than halved in number since the circus moved on to Korea, without the decibel level being affected at all. Duff dribbles around Baraja and Juanfran and slides the ball back to Mark Kinsella, whose shot goes skywards. Keane slices the ball wide after audaciously flicking it over the head of Juan Carlos Valeron. The two teams poke and prod at one another, prying for weaknesses. Matt Holland chases back to hustle the ball off Raul's toe in the penalty box. Then Raul is put through on goal with only the arthritic pace of Staunton to burn off. They lock oars. Staunton matches him inch for inch and uses his shoulder to hold him off while marshalling the ball back to Given. It is masterful defending.

But Spain are beginning to play with great, flamboyant strokes. Halfway through the first-half the ball is in the back of the net again after a beautiful passing movement involving five players. Puyol pumps the ball high into the Irish penalty box. Breen chases backwards to head it, but gets no leverage in his clearance. The ball reaches Morientes on the edge of the Irish box. He plays a neat, cushioned header to De Pedro beside him, then makes a diagonal run into the box, stepping over it as De Pedro plays it to Raul. Trying to keep track of who's gone where has Breen and Staunton looking boss-eyed at one another. Raul flicks the ball with the outside of his right foot to Morientes, who's on the edge of the six-yard box. He heads it back across the face of the goal for Luis Enrique to lift the ball over the diving Given. The linesman's flag is up. Luis Enrique was offside. It is a marginal call.

After half an hour, Spain come close to killing the game dead. De Pedro drops a high cross into the penalty area. Fernando Hierro, the cartoon-faced Spanish captain, arrives to meet it at the back post. Holland has five yards to make up on him. Hierro is pulling back his foot to catch it on the volley when Holland offers up his head as a sacrifice by diving in to nod the ball clear. Breen operates the offside trap with smooth efficiency. The linesman's arm is up and down like a man trying to kick-start his circulation. Staunton, playing as though he knows it's his last day in his country's service, hits another forty-yard pass to within a metre of Duff, who just fails to find Keane with his pass.

Ireland are enjoying most of the possession, but Spain pose too much of a hazard with their rapier-like breakaway for them to commit too many men forward. Duff and Keane are left to forage for themselves. But just before half-time they discover that Spain's defence is far from impregnable. Holland plays a beautifully weighted chip over the top of Hierro and Ivan Helguera. As the ball bounces at shoulder height, Keane, with his back to goal, senses Iker Casillas right behind him and flicks the ball over the head of the Spanish goalkeeper. It clears the bar. But the Irish players leave the pitch with hope.

GIVEN PULLS OFF A CRITICAL SAVE a minute into the second-half. Raul seizes on a mistake by Harte and then, in a blink, turns Breen and Kinsella on the edge of the box and slides the ball through to Morientes. Given tears off his line to block the shot. The match turns on that moment. McCarthy decides that the centre of defence needs shoring up. Staunton is carrying an injury and he takes his final bow, Kenny Cunningham replacing him. Within a minute, Ireland have a chance. Harte hangs the ball high in the box, but it's too near to Casillas who should have little difficulty pulling it out of the air. As he jumps, Kilbane gives Puyol a subtle shove from behind and sends him clattering into the goalkeeper. The ball spills out of his hands and bounces in front of Kilbane, who catches it on the volley. Hierro is back to clear the ball off the line.

More thrust is needed. McCarthy sacrifices Kelly, shifts Duff over to the right wing and puts Quinn on to give Keane someone to play off. The payout comes almost instantly. Quinn begins winning balls in the air and Duff starts terrifying the Spanish defence. Juanfran and De Pedro close in on him. The odds don't bother Duff. He feints to go one way, then sidesteps them both and finds a metre of grass to put in a cross. Within a minute he's at it again. Juanfran again goes out to face him, but with no look of confidence about him. With the ball apparently cemented to his toe, Duff edges closer and closer to him, then drops his right shoulder and is in the penalty box. Juanfran pads after him and lunges in, but carelessly leaves his leg lying around. Duff trips over it. His fall is credible enough to earn a penalty. With clenched fists and barely suppressed smiles, the Irish players quietly celebrate being back in the match. They're not seeing Harte's face. The giant screen behind the goal is unforgiving. The worry lines stand out like contours on a map. He has not had a good World Cup and is in no fit state to take a penalty. He places the ball on the spot, counts six steps backwards, sucks in a lungful of air, breathes out and then hits it. There's no faith in the shot. Casillas doesn't have to extend himself to push it away. It bounces into the path of Kilbane, with the goal yawning wide in front of him, but somehow, inexplicably, he catches the ball with his left shin and balloons it wide from ten yards.

The players aren't disheartened. They push forward again. Jose Camacho, the rotund Spanish coach, sends on Gaizka Mendieta to help Juanfran with the job of stopping Duff and to try to snatch a second goal on the break. Duff has a new toy to play with. He picks up the ball in midfield, embarrasses both his markers with a quick turn and is accelerating clear when Mendieta hacks him down. Mendieta is thinking, 'What else could I do?'

Ireland are committing more and more men to the frontline and living dangerously at the back. With sixty-seven minutes gone, Mendieta gets away from Finnan and put his cross into the six-yard box, though just centimetres too high for Morientes. Raul puts the ball in the net, but Cunningham takes a step forward at the right moment to play him offside. Then another let-off. A free-kick is knocked long into the box. Cunningham claims it, but the ball skews off his head and flies up into the air. He doesn't take his eye off it. When it comes down he jumps for it again, but so does Harte. They get in one another's way. The ball hits Cunningham on the head, then the forearm, and falls in front of Raul, six yards out. He kills it on his chest and tries to flick it past Given with the outside of his right foot. Given saves with his shins.

At the other end, Quinn, Hierro and Helguera are locked in a battle for control of the skies. Quinn is enjoying the most success. Morientes, the goal-scorer, is withdrawn for Albelda, a sure sign that Spain are happy just to hold on to what they have. With ten minutes to go, Duff races to the right touch-line to stop a poor pass from Holland from running out of play. Mendieta goes after him. Duff keeps the ball in play, readjusts his body, ghosts past Mendieta like he's a figment of Camacho's imagination, rounds Albelda and fires a shot that bounces maybe three inches wide of Casillas's right-hand post.

Raul retires injured and Albert Luque arrives in his place. Spain are clinging on. McCarthy responds by adding another player up front, Connolly replacing Harte. With seven minutes to go, Cunningham sends a ball long into the box and Quinn flicks it on with his head to Keane. It's the same position from which he scored against Germany. But the ball bounces high in the air and Casillas is charging at him like a bull. Keane jumps up and tries to lift the ball over him, but is a fraction too late. The keeper blocks it with his arm, the ball is cleared and the two of them end up in a pile on the floor. Keane thinks, 'Was that our last chance?'

There are two minutes left when Mendieta body-checks Finnan on the right. The full-back takes his time over the free-kick, determined to get the trajectory right. He does. It's bound for Quinn's head. By now, Hierro knows he can't get the better of him in the air, so he grabs Quinn's shirt with both hands and tries to put him off his jump. By the time the ball arrives, Hierro has pulled the shirt almost over Quinn's head. The referee points to the penalty spot again. The Spanish protest vehemently, but this one is more clear-cut. With Harte off the field, Keane claims the ball. He puts it down and taxis back five steps, his face a frown of concentration. He runs and hits it, low and to the left. It's a textbook kick. The crowd behind the goal erupts. Keane has done it again, in the last minute. Ireland have half an hour to conjure up a winner.

IT'S BEEN A BAD YEAR FOR MARK KINSELLA. Out for months with injury, he went to Japan knowing that Matt Holland presented a far more compelling case for a place in the team and wondering if he'd be as marginal a figure as the number twelve on his shirt suggested. Then the row happened.

'I have the utmost respect for Roy Keane,' he said. 'I have the utmost respect for Mick McCarthy. Whatever is between Mick and Roy is between them. The decision was Mick's to take. It's funny, but in a way I'm the lucky one out of this whole fiasco. I'm the only one to directly benefit.'

When Keane was gone, he knew that he was the player filling his boots. He shrugged it off. 'It's not like we haven't played without him before. It's been a case of two in, one out for a number of games in the past. There have been times when Roy wasn't available and Mattie and myself came in. Sometimes it was me and Roy, other times it was Roy and Mattie.'

But mostly it was Keane with Kinsella as his adjutant. Now he and Holland were going to have to remember everything they had learned from him. He would play, he said, with the fight of a wounded animal. He was as good as his promise.

THE CHANT IS 'IRELAND, IRELAND, IRELAND', and the momentum is with them too. Duff wanders up the right wing again, with his slovenly gait, dragging the ball behind him. In a wing beat he's gone and Valeron is left kicking at his memory. He plays the ball to Connolly, who can do nothing with it. Eight minutes into extra time, Ireland almost have a winner. Keane is far from home, out on the left side, near the halfway line. He sends a long-distance shot into the penalty area, which the put-upon Juanfran can clear only as far as Holland's feet. Holland chips it into the box and finds Breen, unattended, ten yards out. But Breen makes the error of allowing the ball to bounce and Helguera rushes at him quick enough to convince him to snap at it. The kindest way to describe it is as a defender's shot.

In all the excitement, no one seems to have noticed that Spain have one less man on the pitch. If McCarthy has, he doesn't mention it to his players. Albelda is back on the bench, watching extra time unravel. He's picked up an injury and Camacho has used all of his replacements. Ireland have three strikers on the pitch, Spain only one. But nobody understands why the Spanish are content to play down the clock and take their chances in the penalty shoot-out. The failure to notice their mortal weakness is *the* critical episode on which the match turns.

Spain have chances. Hierro has a volley blocked down and Cunningham puts in a beautifully timed sliding tackle to take the ball from Albert Luque in the penalty box. The action oscillates like a sine curve. Keane has a goal-bound shot deflected away, then Quinn shows up at the wrong end of the pitch to put in a tackle. The Spanish are visibly flustered whenever Duff gets on the ball. Mendieta wrestles him to the floor in the middle of the pitch, then watches, almost in admiration, one winger to another, as Duff climbs back up, the ball still cemented to his foot, and speeds clear of him.

In the second-half, with the match moving inexorably towards a penalty competition, Keane has two chances inside a minute. First, his shot from outside the box is headed over the bar. Then Quinn plays a cushioned header back to him from Cunningham's long ball, but the ball is too close to him when he hits it and it's more than a couple of feet wide. Given plunges low to his right to parry a sneakily spinning shot from Baraja, then Connolly brushes away Helguera's weary effort at a tackle. But Casillas watches, relieved, as the last chance of the match flies past his post.

THE IRISH PLAYERS CONGREGATE in the centre circle, minds slow with exhaustion, and McCarthy walks among them. Harte and Staunton, natural choices for the shoot-out, were substituted and can't take part. Another, Roy Keane, is back home. Instead of choosing his five mentally strongest players, McCarthy asks for volunteers, just as he'd seen his mentor,

Jack Charlton, do at Italia '90. It's a mistake. Charlton had a different set of players. The five who stepped forward against Romania – Kevin Sheedy, Ray Houghton, Andy Townsend, Tony Cascarino and David O'Leary – were older and more worldly-wise than these players. What McCarthy should ask is not 'Who fancies taking one?' but rather, 'Who thinks he can score one?' What Kilbane hears is, 'Who would like to be a hero?' Eager to atone for his earlier miss, he puts his hand up. Like Harte earlier, his confidence is too brittle for him to be successful, but he joins Keane, Holland, Connolly and Finnan on the list of takers.

Keane is first to make the lonely walk from the centre circle to the penalty box. He shakes the tiredness out of his legs and, with supreme indifference to the pressure, puts the ball in the top left-hand corner. Hierro is first up for Spain. He swaggers up to the ball with his long, lazy stride and never looks like missing. His left arm shoots up as he makes contact with the ball, and Given has no chance. Holland places the ball and takes a couple of steps backwards. He takes a short, angular run-up and hits the ball hard and straight. But it rises too quickly, hits the top of the crossbar and bounces over. He buries his face in his hands. Baraja strokes Spain's second home with the side of his foot, and Ireland are behind. Connolly is next, azure eyes locked on Casillas, jaw working over the gum in his mouth. He lays the ball down just in front of the penalty spot, the seasoned penalty-taker's trick to give himself the psychological edge. Connolly took eight penalties for Wimbledon last season and scored every one. His face, though, is that of a man taking his first. He is wracked with nerves and there is no conviction in his effort. He takes a short run-up and side-foots it straight at the goalkeeper. Juanfran can put Spain almost out of sight, but he is in no fit mental state to take a penalty either. He tries to be too clever. He checks his run-up at the last second, allows Given to commit himself one way, then hits it the other. It rolls wide of the post. Nothing in Kilbane's body language suggests he believes he can score. He looks unsure of why he's there. He takes nine steps backwards, then his actions betray his lack of focus. As he begins his run, he wipes his face on his sleeve, a nervous reaction more than an attempt to clear away sweat. His miss comes as no surprise. If Valeron can score Spain's fourth, then Ireland are out. He places the ball calmly, counts his steps backwards and quietly composes himself. He makes the same mistake as Juanfran, faltering at the last moment to try to send the keeper the wrong way. But he outwits himself. His shot hits the outside of Given's right-hand post and bounces wide.

Finnan must score and does, dispatching it high into the top corner. He clenches his fist, but Ireland's fate is out of their hands now. With his kick, Mendieta can put Spain into the last eight. He spots the ball and carefully measures his steps backwards. The referee is unhappy with the position of the ball, though, and tells him to re-spot it. Mendieta obeys and checks that he's happy. The referee nods curtly. Mendieta hits it weakly, his foot scuffing the turf. Given chooses a side and throws himself long at where he's guessed the ball might be. It goes straight and, with almost a contrite look back, rolls over the line. It's finished.

WHETHER YOU FEEL FLUSHED WITH PRIDE or oddly short-changed at the end depends, as ever, on whether you see the glass as half-empty or half-full. The players arrived in Japan a shaken and bedraggled bunch, pledging loyalty to the manager but looking utterly naked without their captain. Damage limitation was the first priority of the matches against Cameroon and Germany. Yet so many of them played above themselves, just as Roy Keane had exhorted them to ever since the night the campaign began. They got through the first round, moved to South Korea, got an unexpected second stamp on their passports and went out on penalties to one of the best teams in the world. They reached the last sixteen and they did it playing football that was easy on the eye.

'As far as I'm concerned,' Mick McCarthy said, 'we're going out of the tournament unbeaten.'

There is no need to speculate about what consolation Keane would have drawn from that. To his eyes, the final audit would show a bottom line of three draws, and a victory over the worst team in the competition. 'You'll never beat the Irish' may have become one of football's eternal truths, but there's a very good chance that you're not going to lose to them either. It was Keane who inspired Ireland to their only significant victory in the two years leading up to the World Cup, and he couldn't bring himself to celebrate it. It was no big deal, he said. We *should* be beating teams like Holland. He had far bigger dreams for this group of players than seeing them become a team capable of drawing with the best in the world.

Yet without him, that is what they became. Many of them played above themselves. Breen, Staunton and Holland delivered performances at the World Cup many thought beyond them. Yet at the same time the players' ambitions shrank. Draws were celebrated like victories. They played with heart and spirit, but for all that still looked lighter without the mad intensity of Keane's desire.

It was the friction between McCarthy and Keane and their different ways of seeing the world that provided the combustion for the engine. Remove one and you're left with an altogether different machine. The team that celebrated the draw with Germany in Ibaraki was functioning on different energy from the one that had beaten Holland in Dublin nine months earlier. But in sending Keane home, a vital component was lost. Keane's brilliance as a player and his brooding disaffection on and off the pitch played as big a part in bringing the team to the World Cup as the loyalty, trust and respect that McCarthy had carefully nurtured among the rest of the players. As much as they needed McCarthy's belief, his respect, his shoulder in difficult times, they also needed a leader out on the pitch who was more stinting with his love, someone they regarded with a quiet fear, someone they would push themselves to any lengths to please. Without either one of them, three draws and a win against a poor Saudi Arabian team was the best they could have expected.

It was, perversely, the dysfunction at the heart of the McCarthy–Keane relationship that made it work. The shame was that the long faultline in their relationship, which they had held together for so long, couldn't have withstood the pressures for a few weeks longer. But it had been clear for almost two years that there were *two* men within the Irish squad who thought they knew how to run things. The team went to the World Cup with two gaffers.

It used to be said that if Keane could have parachuted into Ireland just before international matches and left afterwards without having to speak to anyone, then he would have. Taking him to Saipan, hindsight tells us, was a mistake. In the days before the team set off from Dublin Airport, journalists were openly speculating about how long it would take before he started suffering cabin fever, after a long and frustrating season at Manchester United, away from the wife and children who are the centre of his universe, in the company of a manager he didn't respect and a group of players he felt ambivalent towards, in the searing heat and heavy humidity of a Pacific island, for twenty-four hours a day, with no other distractions. Wiser counsel would have suggested excusing Keane from the first leg of the trip, and he might never have known about the farce over the training base and the 'sure, it'll do' approach to the preparations that so offended his professional pride.

Perhaps McCarthy and Keane could have sat down and discussed an accommodation whereby Keane would have stayed behind in Manchester for treatment on his various injuries and niggles, and then met up with the squad in Japan a week before the tournament began. Maybe they could have sat down in January and said, 'I don't like you and you don't like me. But this summer we're going to the World Cup. It's what you've dreamt of and what I've dreamt of. Let's make an effort to get on and then, when it's all over, we'll never have to look at each other again.' But the tensions that were evident in their handshake after the match against Holland in Dublin, almost a year earlier, went unacknowledged. Non-communication worked for a while. And so did the charms that each brought to the team: McCarthy's positive outlook and his blind faith in a group of players with a genuine love for him; Keane's desire to impose his own manic work rate and standards on everyone else. But it was a marriage of convenience, and two men who pride themselves on speaking their minds had grown tired of pretending long before they ever boarded the airplane for Saipan.

They left behind so many imponderables. Could the team have gone even further than the last sixteen with Keane in it, or was it his departure that galvanised so many players to perform above themselves? McCarthy would say that he took a pick-and-mix selection of some good and some very good players and moulded them into a team that was far better than its constituent parts. They played entertaining football and reached the knockout stages of the World Cup finals. Keane would say that that should have been the base camp of the team's ambitions. He would say, as he had been saying since September 2000, that the players should demand something more of themselves than the moral victory of drawing matches with top international sides. In the end, the country found itself back in the Phoenix Park again, celebrating yet another heroic failure. It's tempting to say that it all unfolded just as Keane would have predicted.

Who is right and who is wrong will be debated long after the next World Cup has come and gone. What is beyond doubt is that the tournament was one of the poorest for many years. France, Argentina, Portugal and Italy were all stripped from the competition early on. Cameroon were a disappointment, Germany one of the most ordinary sides ever to reach the final. Keane would no doubt have considered the group winnable. Then only Paraguay, the USA and South Korea would have barred the team's way to the final. It seems fantastical. Roy Keane's dreams always did.